Raising a Ladder to the Moon

Raising a Ladder to the Moon

The Complexities of Corporate Social and Environmental Responsibility

Malcolm McIntosh

palgrave
macmillan

First published 2003 by
PALGRAVE MACMILLAN
Houndmills, Basingstoke, Hampshire RG21 6XS and
175 Fifth Avenue, New York, N.Y. 10010
Companies and representatives throughout the world

PALGRAVE MACMILLAN is the global academic imprint of the Palgrave
Macmillan division of St. Martin's Press, LLC and of Palgrave Macmillan
Ltd. Macmillan® is a registered trademark in the United States, United
Kingdom and other countries. Palgrave is a registered trademark in the
European Union and other countries.

ISBN 0–333–96270–2 hardback

This book is printed on paper suitable for recycling and
made from fully managed and sustained forest sources.

A catalogue record for this book is available from the British Library.

A catalog record for this book is available from the Library of Congress.

10 9   8   7   6   5   4   3   2   1
12 11 10 09 08 07 06 05 04 03

Editing and origination by
Curran Publishing Services, Norwich

Printed and bound in Great Britain by
Creative Print & Design (Wales), Ebbw Vale

CONTENTS

FIGURES

First Words

The other side

There are two people standing on
opposite sides of a river.
One shouts to the other:
'How do I get to the other side?'
The second replies:
'You are already on the other side.'
(British humorist Eric Sykes' favourite joke)

All our stories are but a story, and this is only another.
Stories should be a mirror held up to life.
Sometimes those mirrors are cracked or opaque.
Only those who look into it can truly know;
you the reader will decide.
(Brian Keenan, *An Evil Cradling*)

Raising a Ladder to the Moon

The title of this book is taken from a letter written by Henry Moriarty, navigator on *The Great Eastern* – the ship that laid the first two trans-Atlantic telegraph cables – in a letter to the Editor of the (London) *Evening Standard* of 7 March 1870.

> It is certain that the originators of the Atlantic Cable, to whom is due the honour of being the pioneers of ocean telegraphy (when their scheme ranked in public opinion, only one degree in the scale of absurdity below that of raising a ladder to the moon) imagined the success would be rewarded by great and permanent remuneration.[1]

The Complexities of Corporate Responsibility

In order to solve problems created by the globalisation project, it is necessary to re-assess some core assumptions, particularly on the nature of our relationship to planet home. When we have re-seen the world we can then re-engage with it *and* ourselves, but at a different level. We must now see people, planet and prosperity in the humbling light of complexity, connectivity and conviviality.

'Raising a ladder to the moon' is a metaphor that was used to describe the immensity of the task of laying the first trans-Atlantic telegraph cable at the end of the nineteenth century. It is used in this book to illuminate the challenges and opportunities that are inherent in the development of corporations as socially and environmentally responsible 'citizens' at the beginning of the twenty-first century.

The globalisation project, in which the world economy acts as one system, has speeded up and become continuous over the last 30 years through developments in communications technology. At the same time humanity has reached a better understanding of the global ecosystem on which the globalisation project is reliant. These two themes are at the heart of this book about corporate responsibility. But as Nobel Prize winning economist Joseph Stiglitz says in *Globalisation and its Discontents*, 'If globalisation continues to be conducted in the way it has been in the past, if we continue to fail to learn from our mistakes, globalisation will not only not succeed in promoting development but will continue to create poverty and instability'.[2]

So how fares the human project of life on Earth? We have succeeded in creating social systems that create *and* destroy, that bind us together in common purpose *and* that set us against one another. Through the development of the scientific method we have succeeded in understanding many aspects of our world. But in this high-speed technological world we have little time to stand and stare. The combination of our current inability to wonder in awe with our obsession with mechanistic detail and our love of scientific rationalism means that we often fail to see the connections between things, between people, and between the planet and ourselves.

Our corporations stand as monuments to our success at building social structures, but we must recognise that they are neither people nor machines. They are alive. They are complex adaptive systems that can take on a life of their own. We need to control them or they and their technologies will control us.

Managing people, planet and prosperity means, to a significant extent, being able to manage our corporations. This book makes reference to many companies – McDonald's, ABB, Deutsche Bank, Coca-Cola, Royal Dutch/Shell, BP, Wal-Mart and others – but particular attention is paid to the Anglo-Dutch monolith Unilever. They bring us everyday products like Dove soap, Axe deodorant, Omo, and now, fish from sustainable sources. Why Unilever? They are big and they are global. They are trying hard to be responsible. But most importantly because perhaps, just perhaps, they have a better understanding of planet home and its social and environmental systems than any government, multilateral agency or non-government organisation. Should we be frightened or overjoyed?

The answer can only be found in looking at the complexity of all situations, not just those involving corporate responsibility issues. We need three perspectives. First is awe, love, faith and openness to beauty. Second is the scientific method. And third, we need to stand back and see things in perspective. The first perspective requires trust, the second analytical rigour, and the third an attitude that can sense the connections between things, between events and between spaces. This requires us to embrace complexity.

In advancing the case for understanding complexity Steven Jay Kline, a mechanical engineering philosopher, says 'our intellectual system is severely fragmented and lacks views of the whole'. In his book *The Foundations for Multi-Disciplinary Thinking* he asks: 'Can we erect overviews of our intellectual enterprise?'[3]

Raising a Ladder to the Moon is my journey towards a more inclusive and comprehensive understanding of the intellectual and practical enterprise of corporate citizenship. Along the way I draw on some of my experiences and how they relate to the developing field of complexity theory, with all *its* complexities and ambiguities. As Gregory Bateson said in his ground breaking book *Towards an Ecology of the Mind*: 'the most important task today is to learn to think in a new way'.[4]

So this book is experiential, analytical and hopefully full of paradox and surprise. Complexity is like that: it throws up the unexpected. As the learning and change philosopher Peter Senge says: 'Sometimes my greatest acts of commitment involve doing nothing but sitting and waiting until I know what to do next'.[5]

The journey begins with my first recognition of corporate behaviour: smelling chocolate from Cadbury's Bournville factory in Birmingham, England, when I was four years old. It concludes with a call for the adoption of a code of humility for all those who claim to know anything. In helping find a way forward, 20 questions are proposed that can be asked at the point of analysis – as a meditation on thinking.

In thinking about corporate citizenship there is a call for humility in our relationships among one another and between the planet and ourselves. In order to reach this state we will have to develop a culture of conviviality so that we can talk across professional and intellectual boundaries. The use of complexity theory will help us to make connections and observe synchronicities that at present may be beyond our imaginations. On this basis we may then be able to take action for change, particularly in how we control and shape our global corporations in the future.

The introduction relates some points in my personal journey from the chocolate factory in Birmingham, England, through an ecological epiphany in a forest in Sweden, to developing an understanding of how globalisation was developing around the world. I was involved in stakeholder consultation, project management and global politics but I didn't know it at this time. As far as I was concerned my experiences were isolated and contained. It was only later that I began to make connections between science, technology, organisations, politics, the planet and 'I'.

Chapter 1 proposes a discussion agenda for the twenty-first century as related to corporate responsibility. It does this through an examination of some of the assumptions we make about our daily lives and about the planet.

Chapter 2 tackles the ecology of corporate citizenship from the perspective of the current discourse in this area of research and practice. What is being discussed and how are companies articulating their sense of responsibility? There are also two examples of the complexities of corporate responsibility in relation to McDonald's in Africa and Unilever globally.

Chapter 3 looks at the paradox of social and environmental responsibility. For sustainability there should be an integrated view of the relationship between the natural environment and social behaviour but, as this chapter points out, there often is not. How is it that we write about major social and political issues without referring back to the planet and the cosmos that nurtures us?

Chapter 4 is about corporate responsibility and complexity. This chapter concludes that many corporate responsibility initiatives would be more successful if they were seen in a wider context, by taking more account of the complexities of situations and by providing space for paradox, surprise and the unexpected.

Chapter 5 provides examples of the application of complexity thinking to corporate responsibility. These examples range from mad cow disease (BSE), to the spread of AIDS, to sustainable town planning, and to developments in corporate governance. It concludes with biomimicry and the comparison of the modern organisation as being akin to a slime mould, with its brains and intelligence on the outside.

Finally Chapter 6 provides 20 questions for analysing any social situation – but particularly issues of corporate responsibility.

Malcolm McIntosh
January 2003
Bath, England

Chocolate, Reindeer and Hiroshima

My earliest memories of corporate life are from when I was age 4 and attended Bournville primary school opposite the Cadbury's chocolate factory in Birmingham, England. I remember that the Cadbury lorries were dark brown, like their chocolate. My mother was sure that too many sweets would destroy our teeth. I can remember from this early age how the Bournville Village was built especially for the people who worked in the cocoa-smelling factory as a community with shops, libraries and doctors, but with no bars or pubs. It had trees, swings and grass to play on. The Bournville Village Trust, established in 1900, is still in existence. It was established to provide workers with 'affordable housing and other necessities of life'. In its first building phase it even provided what was then called 'solar housing' – built with large south-facing windows. For me the words Cadbury, Bournville and Quakerism were synonymous with warmth, comfort, smells and chocolate brown. I was not to know that later my life was to revolve round issues of corporate governance and that responsible enterprises were to provide the content for research, teaching and consultancy for many years. Also, many years later I was to meet Sir Adrian Cadbury, author of many texts on corporate governance, and come face to face with an example of the embodiment of corporate responsibility.

There are moments in life that crystallise and form the backdrop for everything that follows and against which the rest of life is played out. I am fortunate to have lived in England, Sweden, Australia and Japan and to have visited some 60 other countries in pursuit of work, pleasure and learning. As an entrepreneur I have started businesses with no cash, grown community organisations from small seeds, and set up projects in new areas of interest. I have also worked in one of the world's largest and most prestigious organisations, the BBC, spent time investigating one of the world's most cumbersome organisations, the UK's Ministry of Defence, and carried out work for other large organisations, like Royal Dutch/Shell, BP, ABB and Unilever. I have also been seduced by some of the most reputable Byzantine knowledge museums in the world, by which I mean our greatest centres of learning, universities.

In all these places I have been struck by the personal sacrifices in freedom, integrity and happiness that people make to earn a living, which often makes them part of larger communities, even when those communities, as organisations, are sometimes dysfunctional and inhumane.

In 1977, at the age of 20, I was the English teacher for two small towns in the rural heart of Sweden called Leksand and Rattvik. I had just qualified as a teacher in England and had made the decision to try living in Canada or Sweden. It must have been something to do with pine trees, snow and the outdoor life.

Leksand, four hours north of Stockholm by train, sits by the clear, freshwater Lake Syljan in the region of Sweden known as Dalarna. It is where many Swedes take their holidays and is renowned for horses and the paintings of Carl Larsson, recognised throughout the world for representing idyllic children in picturesque natural settings amidst happy wooden houses. It was here that I spent the winter of 1977/8, six very long months of near darkness with two metres of white, white snow. I learnt to ski cross-country, to pimple (fish through the thick ice on the lake), and to consume endless strong coffee and *bullar* (cake) while teaching English. I taught in schools, prisons and in adult evening classes. In rural Sweden evening classes are more an excuse to get together or find a life partner than to learn a language; most of them spoke good English anyway. I did not think then about being part of the globalisation process, but I was, by virtue of promoting the *de facto* global language of international English – a lesser and simpler language than Cockney, New York, Shakespeare, Strine or Delhi.

An epiphany occurred for me when the snow had melted after the long, hard, dark, candle-lit winter. I had grown relatively fit, skiing most days, criss-crossing the frozen lake and pushing myself hard through the surrounding forests. Swedes have a love affair with what they call 'the nature'; a natural affinity that comes from the many months of darkness and the long days of summer. When spring comes they all go mad, some quite literally, with the burst of new life, longer days and the multitude of flowers. During the winter this concern for 'the nature' is matched by their generally high regard for each other. Skiing through the forest, sometimes spotting elk, I was taught that it was important to leave the forest as you found it, for the next skier to experience the same beauty and wonder. This meant dipping well under drooping snow-covered boughs. The forest must be left pristine, like a picture postcard for others – and for yourself the next day. Compare this with the heavy tread of most international tourist developments, with the advertising hoardings that litter the United States, and with the four-wheel drive destruction of some of Britain's areas of outstanding natural beauty.

In spring my hosts, Gun and Tage Alm, took me out for a picnic in the forests that stretched forever around the small town of Leksand. Tage was the managing director and owner of a small factory exporting all over the world, an example of the strength of the Swedish economy. Picnics were always full of good food, schnapps and beer. On this occasion we sat by a small lake in the middle of the forest enjoying the bursting spring and listening to the silence. At one point I picked up a log, as men (and not women) are prone to do, and flung it hard out into the lake. Without saying a word my host stood up, rolled up his trousers and walked out into the lake to collect it. He waded nearly a metre deep into the freezing water and returned to the shore holding my log, which he duly returned to exactly the spot that it came from. I received a gentle but firm admonition: 'Malcolm, we like to leave "the nature" as we find it, for other people and ourselves, and because "the nature" is precious.' This image of trying to tread lightly has stayed with me forever: I can see the picture to this day.

I learnt later of the Buddhist understanding of 'treading lightly on the Earth'. This is central to an understanding of the concept of the ecological footprint of human activities. That day in spring 1978 by a beautiful lake in central Sweden 'leaving "the nature" as you find it' is the picture that helps me hold this principle in my mind.

Some years earlier in the 1960s I rowed for my school on the River Thames in London between Hammersmith and Putney. The water was filthy and smelly and we were always told that if we fell in a stomach pump would be needed to rid the body of toxins and disease. By 1995 the same stretch of river could boast many species of fish. This I have always believed was because of the introduction and enforcement of regulations governing the disposal of waste in the Thames. Where the river had once been seen as an open sewer, now it was incumbent on business, public services and local government to take responsibility for waste matter and to introduce clean technology. Similarly the Clean Air Acts in the United Kingdom have helped to reduce the incidence of smog in British cities that characterised the novels of Charles Dickens and Arthur Conan Doyle – and my childhood.

The theme of water was to appear prominently again when I was working on sustainability and development issues.

Sushi, Hiroshima and science

In 1980 I became director of an English language school in Tokyo, even at that time a mega-city with enormous prosperity. I was thrown into a world of overcrowded trains, of infinite politeness, of the absolute kindness of strangers, of the cleanest, freshest-tasting food, and Japanese management style. As a very young Western manager with Japanese bosses, I had to try to unpeel the many-layered onion that is Japanese culture. I experienced great discomfort and lack of understanding as I stood between a Japanese owner and board and the predominantly British, New Zealand and Australian English language teachers. I had never studied management; I was learning on the shop floor. Much has subsequently been written about 'Asian values', and in particular Japanese management style.

Very rarely has much attempt been made to distinguish between *human* values, specifically *Japanese* values and *Japanese* social customs. I have never found that human values vary much; what I have found is that national characteristics vary a great deal, and that organisational culture is normally a reflection of national characteristics. What is most interesting in all cultures is the distribution of two things: wealth and power.

Fifteen years later, in 1995, one of my Japanese students had risen to become the Vice-President of a large Japanese computer manufacturer. We spent many hours discussing (and laughing about) the problems of managing across national and cultural borders. But one of the points that he made repeatedly concerned the balance between business and humanity. He said: 'We often do business digitally now, in binary, but to be successful we must remember that our customers live in analogue.' In other words, to reduce customers, and other key relationships to units, or to atomise them, or even to attempt to account for them like so many sticks of rock, can result in a lack of understanding and humanity. I often reflect on this as I stand in the checkout queue at the supermarket or read a leading company's CSR report. One can feel very alienated in the supermarket queue, and in the CSR report I can find myself categorised within a stakeholder group I do not recognise.

The Japanese and their food, culture, products and politics have been recurring themes in my life. I can taste *miso shiru* (white fermented soya and fish stock soup) on my tongue, and it belongs to no other country. I was to write a book about Japanese defence policy after 1945, as part of studying for a Master's degree in Peace Studies at the University of Bradford. This book led to a profound and productive period of research and enquiry. I read everything I could get hold of on the development of atomic bombs and the subsequent dropping of 'Little Boy' and 'Fat Man' on Hiroshima and Nagasaki in August 1945. In the wake of the tragedies of BSE (mad cow disease), asbestos, CFC filled aerosols, DDT and other toxic chemicals, and many other technological 'advances' in the twentieth century, the world has at least begun a discussion about the implications of new technology. The 'precautionary principle' is now recognised as a legitimate topic of discussion.

Several lines stand out from an analysis of the atomic bombings on 1945. The use of the language of fertility is the first, and the second is the unstoppability of a scientist in full pursuit of a new line of enquiry.

The two bombs were, according to accounts at the time, named after Roosevelt (Little Boy) and Churchill (Fat Man). Ostensibly the two bombs were dropped because of fears that an invasion of a nearly defeated Japan would increase the number of Kamikaze (suicide) attacks. The Japanese had some 5,000 aircraft and 600 ships readied for such attacks, and the United States had already lost 34 ships, including three aircraft carriers, and 300,000 men in the war in the Pacific. The two bombs fell from the belly of a B52 bomber, named 'Enola Gay' after the pilot's mother. More than 100,000 people died immediately from the impact, with thousands dying from exposure to radiation in the following years. (It is worth noting that in fact greater numbers were killed by US incendiary bombing in the period prior to the dropping of the atomic bombs.)

Much of the language used at the time made reference to myth, birth and fertility. [6] Robert Oppenheimer, the scientific director of the Manhattan project that had developed the bombs, on hearing of the results of the first bomb on Hiroshima, quoted the *Bhagavad-Gita*: 'I am become death, destroyer of worlds'. Churchill said: 'This is The Second Coming in Wrath', and the *New York Times* reported that atomic weapons were 'the first cry of a new born world'. Oppenheimer was made 'father of the year' by the National Baby Institute. He was to espouse the rationale for all scientific work and the development of technology when he said that: 'the reason we did this job (bombing Hiroshima and Nagasaki) is because it was an organic necessity. If you are a scientist you believe that it is good to find out what the realities are.'[7]

When the Second World War was over President Truman spoke of the United States' 'moral certainty' and said:

> We must embark on a bold new program for making the benefits of our scientific advances and industrial progress available for the improvement and growth of underdeveloped areas. The old imperialism, exploitation for foreign profit, has no place in our plans. What we envisage is a program of development based on the concepts of democratic fair dealing.

This connection of science, 'organic necessity', technology, industry and progress was to form the nexus of planetary development in the later twentieth century. It is currently the cause of our unsustainability, but it could be a platform for reaching sustainability if we can only pause and learn the lessons of our industrialised, technologised development on this planet so far. We only need a slight adjustment and we can live in harmony with the planet. This will not remove the angst of existence from our lives; we will continue to ask why we are here and what the purpose of life is. But, as former UK Environment Secretary Chris Patten, now an EU Commissioner, has pointed out, if half the amount spent on ice cream in Europe in one year were spent on clean water globally everyone would have clean water and hygienic sanitation. Only a slight adjustment!

In the late twentieth century I was asked by the publishers Routledge in London to compile sets of archive material from companies that had survived the twentieth century. It was not an elaborate or detailed study but it allowed me to stick my nose into company archives globally. I and a colleague, Ruth Thomas, produced a million-word, nine-volume set of archive material from Levi-Strauss, the BBC, Barclays Bank, BHP, Marks &

Spencer, Royal Dutch/Shell, BP, Rio Tinto and Cable & Wireless. It is worth listing the lessons learnt from the process involved in this archival search:

- While all companies have records, in the form of accounts and legal documents, many companies do not have archives containing both financial accounts and legal documents and related material that paint a full picture of the company.
- Many companies do not have archivists, or related personnel, to whom a request for access to archives can be made.
- Those companies that do have archives have often not catalogued or indexed the materials, thus rendering them inaccessible unless the researcher has a year or two to spare.
- Archive material can be sensitive, but there are no rules regarding prohibitions. In reality this means that companies operate embargoes ranging from five to 40 years.

For every surviving or successful company there will be many more that fail. So what makes for enduring, long-term success? Is it possible to identify the secrets of corporate longevity?

In *Built to Last*, Collins and Porras set out to determine the successful habits of visionary US companies.[8] While their lessons are derived from the United States and the majority of these archival histories are from UK companies, it is worth applying the lessons of their study to this one. For Collins and Porras the notion of a visionary company extends beyond an ability to endure. Crucially, it embraces resilience which they describe as, 'the ability to bounce back from adversity'.[9] Although it was not the intention of their study to seek out companies with 'long lives', they soon observed that their honed sample consisted of companies with an average age of 92 years. To enhance the robustness of their findings the authors analysed their chosen sample against comparable competitor companies. These comparison companies, while successful, had not achieved the high level of success noticeable in the visionary companies. In presenting their findings, Collins and Porras begin by exploding a series of myths that they argue have grown up around successful companies.

From their analysis the authors determined that the beginnings of visionary companies can be far from ideal, if not distinctly inauspicious (the world famous 3M survived and prospered even though it was founded on a failed mining venture). In addition they observed that ideas were often slow to get off the ground. In the archive material we can observe that the founder of the Anglo-Persian Oil Company (which later became the British Petroleum Company), William Knox D'Arcy, obtained permission to explore for oil in Persia in 1901. However his engineer did not discover exploitable reserves until 1908, by which time Ford Motors was already heralding mass production of the Model T. Similarly the first trans-Atlantic cable connecting the United States and Europe telegraphically, laid by Cable & Wireless, broke and had to be laid again. As the navigator on the first cable-laying ship remarked, the travails of being first he thought 'would be rewarded by great and permanent remuneration'.[10] These were hard beginnings, but the brief success of the first cable laid the foundations for its successor.

The greatest surprise from this piece of research is that most companies do not see an understanding of past decision making as a strategic asset. If they do not understand their pasts – and products – then how can we? Perhaps, just as many countries provide access to government files under freedom of information legislation, the same should be done for company archives given their size, scope and role in all our lives. A product such as Omo is as much part of my life as wars, governments and Secretary-Generals of the UN.

There is a strong case for freedom of (or access to) information on corporate decision making.

Reindeer, Siberia and power

In the late 1980s, as a journalist for BBC television working in the *Brass Tacks* team, I was involved in making programmes on social issues such as divorce, rape, social exclusion and the fall-out from Chernobyl on the United Kingdom's Lake District. I also worked on a major series about defence decision making for BBC2. During this period Defence Secretary Michael Heseltine resigned from the British Cabinet, ostensibly in a disagreement with Margaret Thatcher over procurement of helicopters. This was only half the story, and in fact we witnessed a personality clash between two giant Machiavellian egos, Heseltine being prone to spur-of-the-moment grand gestures. Again I was given a real example of the use and abuse of power.

As an antidote to the machinations at the top of the power pyramid, I was also the primary researcher on one of the first television fly-on-the-wall documentary series; this time covering the launch of the last ship on the River Wear in Northeast England. Remembering that in 1900 the Tyne and Wear region of Britain produced 50 per cent of the world's ships, in this series we followed the end of centuries of shipbuilding and the unfolding effect on the local community. It is difficult to conceive of the rise and fall of empires but the changes between 1850, 1950 and 2000 for the United Kingdom give a stark lesson. In the middle of the nineteenth century Britain ruled 20 per cent of the world's population, produced two thirds of the world's coal, five-seventh's of its steel, and over 40 per cent of the entire world output of traded goods.

As the defence economist Malcolm Chalmers has written, the British Empire, or Pax Britannica, was a huge bluff.[11] Under Britain's management the colonies paid for their own oppression, and the British exchequer was a net gainer. This is in complete contrast to Pax Americana, where the net gain is made by US corporations. Britain, to pay for saving itself and Europe from fascism, was forced by the United States in 1950 to open its empire to US business, while attempting to maintain its own global status as a superpower. The development of the global economy and defence and security were to become overarching themes in the literature on corporate citizenship as the complexities of the relationship between business, free trade, ecology and people have become apparent.

Some time after the River Wear programmes I went on to work in the BBC's Natural History Unit in Bristol on programmes that connected human activity with the use of environmental resources, which often led to degradation. In this place I was to meet people whose dedication to protecting the natural environment and whose knowledge of their particular animal, species or habitat was like no other I have met elsewhere.

I arrived at work at the BBC one day in 1985 to find a message from the editor of *Nature* that read: 'Go to Moscow and interview Mikhael Gorbachov about the environment.' Thus, one of the programmes I worked on featured the development of oil and gas reserves in Northeast Siberia in the dying days of the Gorbachov administration. Here I was privileged to spend time with the Nentsy people, who for thousands of years have herded reindeer up and down the Yamal Peninsula. Their lives are deeply rooted in the landscape across which they roam with wooden sleighs, living in tepee-like 'chum' made from reindeer skins. Their clothes are made from the same animal and they collect fish and berries from the local environment as they travel. They tread so lightly, they leave no footprints.

They were pitted against the combined forces of not only of the Soviet government, who wanted to increase their exploitation of the vast oil and gas reserves that lay below the frozen tundra, but also of Western capitalism, which wanted to develop a local petrochemical industry. In the early 1980s the plan was to build the world's largest petrochemical plant on the River Ob at Tobolsk. The project was to be financed by Japan's Mitsubishi Bank, built by the United States's Combustion Engineering (now part of ABB), and managed by Finland's Neste, Europe's largest petrochemical company. Here was global capitalism in partnership with the state trying to find a way forward through dialogue with local community stakeholders. It was a classic tale of multi-local social responsibility meeting the ethics of sustainable development head on.

I spent three winter months criss-crossing Siberia in a one-engine Aeroflot bi-plane interviewing Nentsy tribal leaders, company bosses and government officials. Later I was to appreciate that I had been engaging in a form of stakeholder consultation. Neste had one of the finest environmental records in the world and were anxious not to damage that status, but understood that movements in international politics meant that Finland would inevitably lose its favoured status *vis-à-vis* Soviet oil and gas. They had to move from the sale of primary products to semi-finished plastics.

There were many ironies in the story. The industrial partnership, headed by Neste, ended up in direct dialogue with local environmental groups and the Nentsy. An agreement was reached behind the backs of the Soviet government to establish several small plants and develop capacity among local people. Mikhael Gorbachov left the scene and the Soviet Union collapsed, but Neste, Mitsubishi and ABB all went on to grow in size and become global supra-territorial entities.

Another savage irony was that at one time there was a suggestion that the petrochemical plant might add value by making finished products. These were to be bathroom fittings, including shower cubicles for Japan and Australia. The Nentsy used almost no plastic, and across the whole of the Soviet Union at that time there was a perceived shortage of plastics for anything. Nearly 20 years later Russia is struggling to dispose of discarded plastic and the permafrost of the Yamal Peninsula is melting through global warming.

If trees could talk

Near where I live and work in the southwest of England there are a number of ancient forests. In the Gordano Valley, there is a parish boundary marker tree that is some 600 years old. If this old oak could talk! Near this tree in another forest is a marker stone dating back to the eighteenth century, indicating that this part of the forest had been planted with oak by the Royal Navy, which planned to harvest the timber to make ships over the next 200 and more years. Oak is not ready to use for shipbuilding until it is at least 200 years old. The certainty was that Britain would still need a sail-borne global fleet of ships to manage its empire.

There was no premonition that new technology would make timber, and particularly hard oak, superfluous. The planners of the day also thought that they had to have management systems in place that would withstand changes in personnel, monarchs and international relations. How many of us now make investment or other decisions with an understanding that the perceived benefits will accrue to our children's children's children?

CHAPTER 1

The Complexity of People, Planet and Corporate Responsibility

The relationship between the individual and global corporations is more complex than is sometimes realised. And, more specifically, the relationship between people, planet and corporations is even more complex. Many of us are affluent consumers (I am one) in the early twenty-first century, and this book is about the food we eat, the clothes we wear, the cars we drive, the airlines we fly, the water we drink, who we bank with and the places we live. But in this world, after several thousand years of development, it is also true that 25 per cent of the population are seriously impoverished, and lack minimum provision of food, water, homes and livelihoods, and this in a globalised economy.

At a personal level I have observed four issues at work in human relations. First is how communities and organisations operate; second is how power is used and abused by some people – almost without exception to their own advantage; third is how the first two observations mitigate humanity's closeness – we are essentially all the same; and fourth is how greater consumer affluence tends to lead to a greater distance from an understanding of our personal impermanence and our species extinction.

* * * *

At a macro level there are two issues that dominate international policy and lead to conflict and lack of security: widening socioeconomic polarisation and the problems of environmental constraints.[12] The management of these two issues comes at a time when some commentators point to the 'failure of politics and the erosion of moral values' and 'market fundamentalism having contributed to (that) failure of politics'.[13] How shall we *manage* ourselves in order that poverty and the environmental resource distribution are addressed? What can be learnt from research and practice in different, but related, fields? There are many who argue that this is the century where the people of this planet have to find *shared* values, develop *common* principles and accept *divergent* civilisations if we are to manage our resources for the good of all. As Martin Rees, the UK's Astronomer Royal, has said 'the future could extend into a posthuman era. We're still near the beginning of evolution, not its culmination'.[14]

There are some who argue that sustainability requires us to evolve to a higher plane, or to develop parts of our brains beyond the reptilian. Just as it may be that we cannot 'hear' other intelligences out in space because 'they package reality in a fashion we cannot conceive', so too we may need to repackage reality in order to manage our relations with each other and the planet more equitably.[15]

The events of 11 September 2001 and the collapse of the Enron corporation in December 2001 have focused attention on how we manage conflict and wealth disparity *and* how we manage our private global economic institutions. There are a number of global corporate citizenship initiatives, a range of development programmes and burgeoning consumer economies, but many of the participants in these different but related sectors and activities are not talking to each other, and if they are, they are often talking past each other.

After the cold war we need to learn how to manage the peace. Some commentators argue that the solution is to be found in the way we *see* the world. *Re-seeing* the world will fundamentally determine how we *re-engage* with it.[16] Of particular importance in this context is the manner in which we engage, for the first time, with the Other – those people whose experiences have not been recognised in the story of the world – women, non-whites, non-western cultures, the poor and dispossessed.[17] This process requires both learning and *un*learning, networking ideas across traditional boundaries and taking action for change.

An examination of the complexity of corporate social responsibilities involves an interdisciplinary approach. This means:

- Taking in international policy, specifically related to poverty, gender and development.
- Management and business, specifically related to corporate social and environmental responsibility.
- Education, specifically related to learning and personal, community and organisational change.

- Development, peace and conflict studies, specifically related to regions in conflict, transitional economies and developing countries.
- Technology, specifically related to the development of science and the relationship between technology, science and capitalism.

There is a need to learn how to manage the peace. There is a global industry built round research and teaching programmes on business administration (MBAs).[18] The global elite may have learnt how to manage global finance, build multinational corporations and develop consumer economies, but have not been as successful at managing peace, resolving conflict and establishing stability. There is a need to understand how we manage and nurture social capital – that most vital of resource in all societies – particularly in transitional economies, but also in all communities, local and global. And there is much that humanity still has to learn about its relationship to planet home.

There is much to be gained in research and practice through an interdisciplinary approach to the management of peace, security and ecological sustainability. Managers in multinational corporations, officials in public administration and workers in civil society organisations often find themselves managing in regions of conflict and involved in dispute resolution but without the necessary skills or competencies to work across traditional sectoral and intellectual boundaries.

Despite the growth of a 'new social partnerships' approach to sustainability, accountability and development issues, there is much that can be gained from developing research that reaches into the literatures on and experiences of business management, development, international policy and peace studies. At the same time understanding how managers in private business, public policy and civil society can work more closely together requires new approaches to learning and change.

The distracted self and empty meaning

Before e-mails and mobile phones, even before fax, the poet T.S. Eliot wrote of the 'distraction by distraction' and 'time-ridden faces . . . filled with fancies and empty meaning'.[19] Today, like the other days of the week, I will receive up to a hundred e-mails, while my voice-mail box will be stuffed and my post box overloaded. Whereas once people paused awhile before opening their mouths or putting pen to paper, now contact is like junk fast food: continuous, low quality, full of extraneous crap and bad for you. As psychologist Kenneth Gergen has written: the 'massive increment in social stimulation – moving toward a state of saturation – sets the stage for radical changes in our daily experiences of self and others. . . . With social saturation the coherent circles of accord are demolished.'[20] What is my identity and what do I believe? Who am I and why am I here?

Like many people I am part of a growing global elite class – downloading e-mails, working with colleagues in four continents, owing allegiance to my airline/supermarket/oil company reward card, rarely using cash, mixing croissants with sushi, and watching global TV.

We used to say that we spend a third of our lives asleep; now it is possible for a significant elite to say that they spend part of their lives at 35,000 feet – maybe asleep, but often working away at the laptop. Despite the events of 11 September 2001 air travel is expected to grow, particularly among Joe Public on cheap, no-frills airlines in the United States and Europe.

Meanwhile, 35,000 feet below, 25 per cent of the world's population will not see the age of 40, living on less than US$1 a day and fighting over the most meagre of resources. I am reminded that on average it takes 6 litres of fossil fuel to deliver one kiwi fruit to a British supermarket, and that one trans-Atlantic return flight has the same environmental impact per person as driving a car for a year.

The economy of Bath in the southwest of England, where I live, is dependent on three sources of income. First, it is a significant retail centre and goods come from around the world; second, it is a tourist honeypot, with visitors coming mostly from the United States, Japan and the United Kingdom; third, as elsewhere in the United Kingdom, illegal substances are consumed openly by many people here, and by much of the rest of the population of the United Kingdom on a regular basis.[21] It is all good business for Bath, a city with a 2000-year history of alternative lifestyles, health, happiness and hippiness.

The local bank manager is happy to bank money from hotels, petrol stations *and* a number of local drugs dealers. One of them, Jon, operating with several co-workers, has a 'good' business with a turnover of £500,000 a year. He manages a chain of street dealers selling illegal drugs.

Banks are also part of the informal economy. Domestic cleaners are paid in cash: 'its so much easier, and then I don't have to pay tax', people say. Lunch is eaten at restaurants where the food is cooked and served by a 14-year-old who earns far less than the statutory minimum wage and has had no food hygiene or health and safety training. It is a low inflation, high employment, cash economy. Boomsville Bath and Britain: the epitome of the 'benefits' of globalisation.

Corporate citizenship is an elephant

Many teachers in the management field are fond of using the Hindu parable of the six blind men who encounter an elephant. After a seemingly shared experience they all recount different understandings of their meeting. One said it was soft, one high, one warm, one moving, one like a tree, one did not know what to make of it. There are many versions of this story and they all vary, but there are two constants: there is something to be experienced and there is something to be said.

Corporate citizenship is an elephant. Elephants: you wonder at their immensity, at their wisdom, at their societies, at their babies, at their age, and at their history, and I guess some people eat them. Corporate citizenship is also like 'a ladder to the moon', the title of this book. It has a sense of the unreal, the illusory, the absurd. For some it is mission impossible; for others an obvious metaphor for the new role and responsibilities of business in society.

If we postulate that corporate citizenship is something to do with the relationship between organisations and people and planet, where should we start? When asked what it was I did ('corporate citizenship'), and I duly answered, friends and neighbours lost concentration after a few seconds of explanation. Academic colleagues gave me their versions of what they thought I *ought* to be working on. Journalists wanted something short and pithy, like a strapline or a marketing catchphrase. So I am used to saying: 'it's about the relationship between business and society, or it's about social responsibility – yunno, looking after the environment and communities'. The easiest answer I have discovered is: 'It's about decision making and governance – how decisions are made and by who for whom.' This seems to find resonance with everybody: friends, researchers and journalists. I suppose people like the idea of understanding more about who is managing their lives.

This attempt to see the world through an examination of the role of business in society is an attempt to give meaning to what is seen and felt. The starting point is corporate social responsibility, sometimes known as corporate citizenship, and various attempts to make the powerful (people, governments and organisations) accountable for their actions, to make them more open to scrutiny, and make good governance a feature of the landscape.

Let us not be fooled; corporations are not citizens. They are not people; they have been created by people in their own image. The term corporate citizenship is only ever a half-useful metaphor, and is no truer than that 'Omo washes whiter'. Corporations and governments often claim to wash whiter.

All our institutions are under scrutiny, and none more so than corporations. The world of corporations is challenged by increased stakeholder activism, by the democratisation of information and by corporations seeming inability to conduct themselves honestly and humanely.

Walking down the high street, turning on the television, picking up the newspaper: at first sight there is a jungle before me of brands, corporations, issues and dilemmas. Making meaning entails finding some order in the apparent chaos. For instance here are some pieces of seemingly fragmented information:

- The world's best selling soap is called Dove.
- Eight of the world's largest companies earn between them more than half the world's population.
- Twenty per cent of the world's people live on one dollar a day.
- McDonald's serve 0.1 per cent of all the food served every day on planet Earth to humans.

Standing and staring, it is possible to identify some connections between these seemingly dissociated pieces of information. Rather than random chaos, patterned complexity emerges. In the patterns that emerge there are some moral issues. In the ensuing debate about cause and effect, about the state of the planet and humanity, it is possible to see that we could decide as one race to evolve to a higher level of understanding and live in harmony with the planet and each other.

The attempt to find meaning is perplexing some days, and other days so apparently full of clarity that every bite transports the soul. But the search for meaning also leads to two points. One is pure peace and absolution: I am sorry for all my sins and content with who I am. I am being here now and it is heaven on Earth. The other search for meaning on corporate social responsibility is frustrating: I am confronted by a series of contradictory messages. If I let the advertising transport me I am bound to be a discontent, for they raise my expectations too high: apparently my shirts will be whiter and my bank balance fuller. But if I answer all my e-mails I will have no time to clean my teeth, chew the fat or stroke the cat. Everything I ever wanted to know is here on my screen. Type in Einstein (Google: 1.83 million hits for Einstein: 14 October 2002) and he is alive in my living room along with the new sofa I downloaded from the net.[22] As Scottie from *Star Trek* didn't say: 'beam me down a three-piece suite'. And yet to function personally and professionally I must say something that seems to mean something: that goes beyond knowingness, that tickles fancies.

I am only too aware of how my senses are flooded, of how technology has become more powerful than our ability to understand it, how science and morality are running hard to keep up with the waves of information, how I am besieged by the sharp spikes of quick global contact, and how I am overwhelmed by plastic bags of ephemerality loaded with instant wafer-thin celebrities.

And yet life is about drives and aspirations, without which there is nothing. Why get up in the morning? Two survivors of the Nazi concentration camps in the first half of the twentieth century, Victor Frankl and Bruno Bettelheim, said it was about 'there being something more to do' and about 'devising strategies for surviving'.[23]

We have striven to create order out of chaos; but humans are destined to be eternally at the edge of chaos in the space between order and freedom, between the predictable and the dynamic.

The unfathomable wordless void

I am standing next to a waterfall and the sound is immense as thousands of litres of water crash from the rock shelf above into the pool below. I know there is a river and a waterfall and I can see the spray sparkle in the sun. As I focus on the fall and the wet I can feel the energy of the moment and I am temporarily as one with the river, floating, then crashing, then meandering towards the sea. It is the movement of the moment that consumes me.

Music can have the same effect. Abdullah Ibrahim is a black South African jazz pianist, best known previously as Dollar Brand. One of the aspects of his music that he is best known for is the silence he creates, for the space between the notes. Other musicians make similar comments. Classical pianist Arthur Schnabel said 'the notes I handle no better than many pianists, but the pauses between the notes – ah, that is where the art resides!' Just so with Ibrahim, who lived in exile from South Africa between 1976 and 1990. In an interview in 1988 he spoke of the silence of the oppressed and of dynamism: 'We are homesick for a democratic society, the society of South Africa for all the people, regardless of race or creed.' His musicians 'become like actors interpreting the feelings of the voiceless in South Africa. They have been forced into silence. We report their pain and their courage. . . . Improvisation has to do with fearlessness of the unknown.'[24]

The management of the modern corporation has similar characteristics to Ibrahim's music and the energy of the waterfall. We are surrounded by energy and moments between actions; it is what we make of the energy and the action that provides the dynamic. In the case of the successful corporation, it is the difference between success and failure. In the case of global society, the modern corporation can use the force to destroy or to enable the recognition of the common good. As the *I Ching*, written some thousands of years ago, said (and this could be true also of any community of people, even corporations):

> We shape clay into a pot,
> but it is the emptiness inside
> that holds whatever we want.

In *The Emperor's Nightingale*, Robert Monks has written that until recently he saw the corporation as 'a machinelike system increasingly based on non-dynamic, non-living, non-human principles: a profit-seeking missile of unlimited life, size, and power operating under the stealth of human guise'.[25] Now, with the advent of various innovative local and global governance initiatives, he has come to find hope in a re-analysis of corporations as living complex adaptive systems: as agents that can have the potential to enhance humanity.

There is a link to be made between seeing the world as a complex place and the power we have vested in some of our largest economic institutions: private corporations and nation-states. If we can just stand back, we can see the world not as near-entropic chaos but as adaptive and dynamic. Within this rich picture our institutions can be seen as social systems that could work within an inclusionist view of life in space and on Earth. For Earth is currently home to humanity.

Corporations and others need only make small, but distinctive, changes in order to show courage and leadership, but this requires more time for reflection – time to stand and stare. *What assumptions am I making that I don't know I'm making?* is probably the most useful question to ask everyday.

Ben Zander, leader of Boston Symphony Orchestra, and his wife, the psychologist Rosamund Stone Zander, have said that the job of a leader is not to make decisions. It is to make 'distinctions'.

The discipline of making distinctions is based on two questions: *What assumptions am I making that I don't know I'm making, and what can I create that will give me something new?* Making distinctions is about performing small, inventive acts – acts that are totally different from normal strategizing or scheming. Leaders of the future will create categories that give people information on how to do their jobs and on how to live their lives. . . . Never doubt the capacity of the people you lead to accomplish whatever you dream for them. It's a principle that leaders like Gandhi, Martin Luther King and Nelson Mandela have all embodied. Imagine if Martin Luther King had said, 'I have a dream – I wonder if people will be up to it?'[26]

Hope and planet home

The assumption that has been made up until now, and certainly since the birth of industrial capitalism, is that planet Earth's resources are bountiful and her carrying capacity is infinite. This assumption includes the chartering and incorporation of our corporations. The argument has been that capitalism is naturally good and that in order for its corporate agents to function they should be allowed to externalise significant proportions of their risks. But, now that our corporations have grown so big, and some of them so scornful of humanity, the complex global adaptive system – the ecosystem – may see fit, not out of malice or foresight or predictability, to adapt and re-balance. This may not be good for humanity in the long run, and is certainly not good for some 25 per cent of humanity immediately.

It should be possible to pause awhile, to stand and stare. While we stand and stare we should examine three things:

- What do we now know about the adaptability of our global ecosystem?
- What do we know about our technical and technological systems?
- What have we learnt about social systems?
- And, most important, what have we learnt about the relationship of these three?

The systems are all adaptive, and they are all complex, but the ecosystem may adapt in such a way as to diminish the life fulfilment expectations of an even larger proportion of humanity. Most important is to see these three distinct areas of reductive analysis as symbiotic, as inseparable in reality, as integrated parts of a whole.

Thinking of air as water

The fundamental problem of sustainability is that there has been a failure to understand the complexity of life on Earth. This is because of the tendency to divide and reduce analysis to component parts. If we looked at the relationship between things rather than at things themselves, we would see that things only have meaning by virtue of context. It is the spaces between things that give meaning to life and lend possibilities for dynamism, action and change. It is in the silence of space that we will hear ourselves. And 'space' is a misnomer; we are talking about relationships and connectivity. It is no wonder that there is so much synchronicity about. A fungal specialist, microbiologist Alan Rayner, has written that our problem is that air is too thin: we take it for granted. If we think of ourselves as swimming in water (and the chemical difference between air and water is not too great) then we will feel the connectivity more distinctly. This analogy will be most apparent to anyone reading this at 8000 metres: you are hoping that the air has some density and connectivity and that gravity prevails. The former means that you should have a smoothish ride and the latter that your plane does not fly off into space. So, some fundamental rationalist scientific understanding is, in this case, reassuring (personal communication).

Management, humanity and soul

In order to beat the blues that accompany postmodern deconstruction, it is good to have a positive agenda, a way of going forward. Here is a vision from UN Secretary-General Kofi Annan in 2000:

> We have to choose between a global market driven only by calculations of short-term profit, and one which has a human face. Between a world which condemns a quarter of the human race to starvation and squalor, and one which offers everyone at least a chance of prosperity, in a healthy environment. Between a selfish free-for-all in which we ignore the fate of the losers, and a future in which the strong and the successful accept their responsibilities, showing global vision and leadership. Let us choose to unite the powers of the markets with the authority of universal ideals.[27]

And here is a way of seeing the world from two people: a management theorist and a Marxist poet:

> The activities of corporations are no longer defined by the imposition of abstract command and the organisation of simple theft and unequal exchange. Rather, they directly structure and articulate territories and populations. They tend to make nation-states merely instruments to record the flows of commodities, monies, and the populations they set in motion. . . . This is really the new biopolitical structuring of the world.[28]

Zygmunt Bauman argued in *Post-modern Ethics* that postmodernism, rather than divorcing us from choice by throwing us into a fragmented, nihilistic place of uncertainty, called on us to examine our moral choices more closely.[29] He argued that the modern world requires a greater concentration of moral effort because we can no longer accept the universal truths of the past. So, in line with Kofi Annan's statement quoted previously, perhaps the best place to begin is with the world as it could be. Here is the Dalai Lama speaking to the European Parliament in September 2001:

> Today's world requires us to accept the oneness of humanity. We must learn to work not just for our own self, family or nation, but for the benefit of all humankind. Universal responsibility is the best foundation for personal happiness and for world peace.

Approaching the subject of corporate citizenship from disparate angles means not assuming that it is easy to identify heroes and villains – personal or corporate. It does not assume that we know where we are going. It *does* assume that humans share similar conditions. We share the same delicate, beautiful, intricately balanced planet twirling through space. We share the same cosmic angst, never quite sure why we are here. We share our humanity and all our pasts, presents and futures. We have one soul and one collective unconsciousness.

On this basis, the themes that now seem to present themselves in the field of corporate citizenship, that have lead to the thoughts in this book, are:

- The relationship between human activity and the natural environment, represented in the debate around sustainable development.
- Governance and accountability for, and transparency in, decision making in business and government.
- The contrast between talking to people and talking to organisations, and the disconnect that occurs.
- The relationship and discourse (and lack thereof) between the corporate business world, public policy making and local communities.
- The development of networks, network organisations and universal values, and the clash with places and territory.

- The use and abuse of power, and the apparent power vacuum in many contemporary global–local situations.
- And, most confusingly, that sometimes things just seem to happen without due rhyme or reason. Either this means that nobody is willing or able to take responsibility or that the most powerful force is at play: synchronicity.

Synchronicity arises because of the complex patterns that emerge from an examination of any situation. And this is where this book finds its conclusion. We are swimming in water. Radar in the 1940s proved this, and mobile communications today ought to convince us of our connectivity.

CHAPTER 2

The Ecology of Corporate Citizenship

There are perhaps two normative answers to the question: 'What is corporate citizenship?'

- Organisations should understand their social and environmental impact, as well as their financial performance.
- Organisations should understand their role, scope and purpose, and be able to articulate them.

And there is one overriding statement regarding the reorientation of the debate over corporate social responsibility. Whether they like it or not corporations are public culture: they are of us (political and social and economic).[30] This is not a debate over private property rights, but a concern with how we manage the planet. Some of our largest economic institutions are market driven organisations. This book is about them – and us.

The debate

Companies, consultants and others in the corporate citizenship movement devote a great deal of energy to understanding and establishing criteria for measuring the social and environmental impact of organisations. These are attempts to rationalise the world and provide managerial instrumentalism, and thereby reassure themselves and stakeholders. A similar amount of energy is devoted to establishing and attempting to articulate the vision and values of organisations. There is much mileage to be gained in working on these parallel tracks, and there is a healthy profession developing.

Much of the well-meaning work in these areas fails in two respects, however. First, there are many in the business community who are not convinced that this conversation is anything more than hot air; a waste of time, detracting from the core business of business, which is to make money and reward the nominal owners: the shareholders. Second, much of the debate takes place in a contextual void with little, or no, reference to the rest of society.

The debate about the role, scope and purpose of business, sometimes called corporate social responsibility and at other times called corporate citizenship, often starts in the wrong places.

There is a popular perception that, if there are villains, it is companies that are the villains of the piece. Then there is a perception that if we only make companies accountable then control will be gained over their nefarious activities. This may be true, but we need to look elsewhere for the answers.

Much of the writing on corporate citizenship focuses on recognisable *corporate* behaviour, which is easily observable, while a great deal of what is actually happening is either in the realm of the processes of the market, or in the realm of illegitimate, informal or illegal activity – in other words *unincorporated* market behaviour. We live in a society of organisations *and* networks and this poses enormous ethical questions about 'whose values are they anyway: ours or theirs or nobody's?' But our lives are shaped by a faster and faster moving continuum of superficial contact. Ephemera and instant celebrity rule! It is difficult to pin down what *is*; as the authors of *Funky Business* expressed so well. 'Crash! Boom! Bang! Welcome to the age of accidents. Welcome to the age of constant alarm bells where surprise is all and no one can predict what will happen tomorrow.'[31]

It is also important to look at corporations *and* brands. In other words we may need to look downstream and think about *brand citizenship,* as well as corporate citizenship. Corporate citizenship is fraught with dangers and ambiguities. For example, Virgin is one of the largest companies, selling to everyone around the world. They sell banking, airline tickets, music and drinks. It is possible, although perhaps boring, to live a Virgin life. Perhaps my tribe is Virgin? Do our brands and our corporations represent our yearnings to find identity?

Should we start with the corporation or with citizenship, given that citizenship is not even a common expression? After all most people do not think of their local supermarket or their bank as a citizen.

There is much written about the social and environmental impact of large business organisations, and this is not new. What is new is that we cannot decide whether they are a good or bad thing; we cannot decide if they are in control of our lives or not; whether they are honest or not; whether our politicians have control of them.

There is no doubt that the world has been restructured since 1945 around markets and market-based organisations and institutions. Some of these, such as the UN and its 'family' of agencies, being the only global political bodies that we have, are radically challenged by a market-dominated world.

It is a truism that we *share* one world and we can, if we wish, *manage* decisions collectively to shape that world in the future for the benefit of all humankind. How this century develops will depend on whether we can recognise shared values, on developing common strategic principles and our ability to *accept* (if not necessarily celebrate) divergent civilisations. Three overlapping and symbiotic institutional processes now dominate the world: private corporations, the state and civil society. It is often the case that there is a clash between the three.

If the dilemma is about values, responsibility and purpose, then Benjamin Barber is right when he says that the focus in this debate should be on active collaboration. 'Civic responsibility is a partnership between government, civil society and the market. It necessarily depends on the active collaboration of political leaders, citizens and business people.'[32]

International cross-currents

Australia used to be known as a meat and dairy exporter, and this is still a significant source of income, but just as they used to brand cattle and sheep they are now branded themselves – for life. More than 80 per cent of Australian supermarket sales come from just ten companies, all of them domiciled elsewhere. Markets? Choice? Where? And this is despite the fact that in polls away from the checkout tills Australians claim to care about the companies they buy from, and care about the products they buy. According to a Millennium Poll 45 per cent of Australians think that 'large companies should set higher ethical standards and help build a better society'.[33]

In Sweden, corporate citizenship sounds like a good idea, because *of course* companies should be socially responsible, there is no need for business to be involved in the provision, or indeed any debate concerning the provision, of public services as these services are provided by the state. In Denmark also, with some of the highest personal rates of taxation in the world, there seems to be contentment with the clearly separated roles for corporations and the state, and the significant role for civil society. Copenhagen recently came top of a list of the best cities in the world to live in.

On a BBC Radio programme in the United Kingdom involving myself and representatives of the Institute of Directors, the Transport and General Workers Union and a columnist from the right-of-centre *Times* newspaper, the *Times* columnist argued that stakeholder governance, as opposed to shareholder governance, was akin to fascism. The argument ran like this: 'Governments gain their legitimacy from their electorates and companies from their shareholders, but stakeholders have no legitimacy and no mandate.' What are we to make of the 1.1 million members of the UK's Royal Society for the Protection of Birds, or Greenpeace International's 1.2 million global membership or Amnesty International's more than a million members worldwide? Most political parties would love to have that number of committed members, and any company would be in heaven if it had a million committed customers.

At a State of the World Conference in Dublin in 1999 the CEO of a major US corporation, having sat through three days of discussion on the role of business in international development, rose to his feet to thunder: 'I am fed up with all this discussion about stakeholders – what about customers!' As if customers and stockholders are not stakeholders.

The ecology of corporate citizenship

It is always a surprise when teaching business and management students on international MBAs and other business programmes around the world to be faced with multiple understandings of the role of business in society, to such an extent that much of the first session is preoccupied with: 'Give me a clue as to what this corporate citizenship thing is?' Being asked 'What is the purpose of business or what is the corporation for?' comes as a profound shock to many students. We do not have a tendency to ask fundamental questions about our society, particularly where business and management are concerned. But our future may depend on our asking what our corporations are for and if they are the best way of delivering what we want.

The feeling that we do not ask the questions that matter most is echoed by best-selling author Stephen Covey who says: 'Ask people what the purpose of the company is and you'll get ten different answers. They're not on the same page. They don't know the purpose of the company.' The discussion of corporate citizenship is traditionally set within the boundaries of management theory, international policy, organisational behaviour and ethics. Its ecology is therefore bounded by discussions that sometimes contradict its integrated or holistic approach to market-driven private organisational behaviour. As Paul Hawken wrote in *The Ecology of Commerce*, his book's title 'reads as an oxymoron' because of 'the gap between how the earth lives and how we now conduct our commercial lives'.[34] This chapter has the same problem. The way our international corporations have developed may not augur well for our ability to tackle the conflict that now arises from the global wealth disparity and problems over environmental resources.

The end of one century and the beginning of another produces many summations of the development of the human race, if you accept the millennial dating system. There is also 'endism' afoot which postulates at every turn that it's 'the end of history', 'the end of nature' or 'the end of modernity' – and, of course, the end of the millennium! However, one theme is common to, and seemingly shared by, most commentators at present. It is perceived that there is a global disconnection between finance, trade, business organisations and social and environmental conditions. One of the things that the corporate citizenship agenda seeks to do is marry these issues; in particular using the organisational power that lies in corporate hands to effect the management of global capitalism alongside global social development.

For George Soros, a significant beneficiary of open global markets, 'open society is endangered' by 'the crisis of global capitalism'. His prescription is that 'market discipline needs to be supplemented by another discipline: maintaining stability in financial markets ought to be the objective of public policy'.[35] For the corporate citizenship movement, it is the maintenance of stability in the social market as well as financial markets that is of paramount importance. Barnet and Cavanagh have an agenda not dissimilar to Soros's, arguing that 'bringing global economic institutions under the authority of political institutions is essential to protect the environment, human rights, and job possibilities around the world'.[36] This is echoed by the UN Secretary-General's call for business to help 'give a human face to the global market'.[37]

There has been a spate of books attacking the economic monoliths of modern life: private corporations. They apparently are the principle architects (or the result) of the dissonant relationship between economics, society and the environment. Some of the titles tell all. Noreena Hertz's *The Silent Takeover* is subtitled *Global Capitalism and the Death of Democracy*; Richard Welford has written *Hijacking Environmentalism: The Corporate Response to Sustainable Development*; Naomi Klein's *No Logo* is subtitled *No Space, No Choice, No Jobs, No Logo: Taking Aim at the Brand Bullies*; and David Korten's books include *When Corporations Rule The World*.[38]

Embrace the dead donkey

This is one of many post-Enron collapse jokes. It is based on a paradox and the unexpected.

A city boy, Kenny, moved to the country and bought a donkey from an old farmer for $100. When the farmer came the next day to deliver it, he delivered the bad news that the donkey had died. Kenny had a bright idea.

'Give me the donkey,' he said, 'and I'll raffle him off.'

'You can't raffle off a dead donkey,' the farmer replied.

'Sure you can, if you don't tell anybody he's dead.'

A month later the farmer met up with Kenny and asked, 'What happened with that dead donkey?'

'I raffled him off, selling 500 tickets at $2 each for a profit of $898.'

'Didn't anyone complain?' the farmer asked.

'Just the guy who won,' Kenny said. 'I gave him back his $2.'

Kenny grew up to become the CEO of Enron.

This attack is representative of the growing frustration felt by those who face the anonymity of corporate power. But it fails to address three important issues. First, *some* corporations advance global social development. Second, the oppression and lack of social and environmental justice suffered by many people is caused by institutional actors other than business: a mixture of governments, UN agencies, military associations and other multilateral systems. Third, the growth of global private corporations has been due to the vacuum in global social governance. In other words we have the corporations we deserve because, like technology, they have developed at a pace greater than our ability to hold them to account. Fourth, critics on the left and the right agree that business has failed in the main to articulate its role, scope and purpose. This is true of David Henderson and those who have written about new initiatives such as the UN Global Compact.[39] That different commentators should be in agreement on this issue indicates a serious market failure!

Thinking about corporate citizenship

A private corporation is an organisation formed by people making use of resources; it has limited financial liability and the ability to act as a person and to transfer ownership between shareholders. This definition is helpful but limited. It highlights several problems for modern society, and (for some) it clarifies the current legal role of the private corporation. Giving the corporation a personhood, but also limited liability, is akin to giving a real person the sanction to rape and pillage without holding them accountable. Limited liability can mean that sometimes shareholders simply do not care, as long as they are financial beneficiaries.

It is true that many directors of companies do abuse society through their abuse of company law, but increasingly we are witnessing a further clarification of the company as a vehicle for enterprise with the common good in mind. This movement is being enacted through changing regulations regarding company governance, reporting and behaviour, through governments' use of economic instruments to steer corporate behaviour, and in the development of voluntary initiatives and partnerships between different actors in society with compatible values and aims.

It can be argued that the growth of corporate citizenship is an area where research has followed practice over the last ten or so years. Even so the reasons for the upsurge in interest, either theoretical or practical, have not changed in that period. In the early 1990s it was said that they were:

- growing environmental awareness
- the development of equal opportunities
- exposure of corruption and fraud
- increasing organisational transparency as a result of information and communications technology
- stakeholder empowerment
- the evolution of free market economics as the dominant global economic system
- the need to engage with, and report to, a range of stakeholders on issues beyond compliance and financial and obligations, and
- good management practice.[40]

This is also represented in Figure 1, which shows a ripple effect of the company's impact that includes economic, social and environmental impacts.

'Citizenship is the most privileged form of nationality', according to one definition, and implies reciprocal rights and responsibilities between the state and the individual.[41] The development of citizenship as a counter to the absolutist power of monarchs or feudal land owners has been hard won and should perhaps not be watered down by being used as a metaphor to describe the relationship between corporations and society. Some commentators argue that, like limited liability, the use of the term citizenship is a misnomer and is abused by company directors hiding behind its apparent acceptance of moral purpose. There is also a school of thought, developed from Milton Friedman's Chicago School, that the inherent sense of social responsibility embedded in the term corporate citizenship is a distraction from the real purpose of business: to make private wealth. In particular David Henderson has written that:

> CSR (corporate social responsibility) is flawed in its prescription as well as its diagnosis. What it proposes for individual businesses,

through 'stakeholder engagement' and giving effect to 'the triple bottom line', would bring far-reaching changes in corporate philosophy and practice, for purposes that are open to question and with worrying implications for the efficient conduct of business.[42]

Henderson lays blame for this new social agenda for business at the door of business. 'International business shows a reluctance or inability to argue a well constructed case for itself against unjustified criticism and attacks.' Perhaps critics such as Henderson should examine carefully the arguments emanating from companies such as Unilever, Royal Dutch/Shell, BP and others. They have articulated carefully how they see their role in global development. There are flaws in their arguments, but

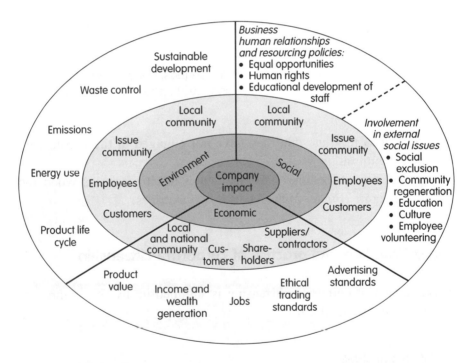

Figure 1. Ripple effect

Source: Taken from J. Andriof and M. McIntosh (eds) *Perspectives on Corporate Citizenship* (Greenleaf Publishing, 2001), page 15. Reproduced with permission.

		LEVEL OF ANALYSIS	
		Local, community or national scope	**Global or universal scope**
UNIT OF ANALYSIS	**The individual person as citizen**	**Cell 1: the invididual citizen** Relationship of the person to the state; rights and duties of citizens; national and cultural identity	**Cell 3: the universal citizen** Common humanity; interdependence; universalism; less grounded in fixed rules or laws; asserted based on philosophical ideas
	The business organization as citizen	**Cell 2: the corporate citizen** Business as a responsible player in its local environments; emphasis on voluntarism and charity, as well as on the organisation's rights and duties in and for the community	**Cell 4: the business citizen** Business as a responsible local actor and a consistent global actor; emphasis on the organisation's rights and societies within and across national and/or cultural borders; there is a need for analyis of hypernorms

Figure 2. Four states of citizenship

Source: Taken from J. Andriof and M. McIntosh (eds) *Perspectives on Corporate Citizenship* (Greenleaf Publishing, 2001), page 87. Reproduced with permission.

it is ridiculous to argue that they have not engaged in the debate with reasoned submissions.

A useful way of looking at different states of citizenship is Wood and Logsdon's figure (Figure 2), which uses two matrices.

The articulation and practice of corporate citizenship

The dilemma of corporate citizenship is summed up by five companies that lay claim to practise it.

Cable & Wireless

Cable & Wireless is a global telecommunications company founded in 1872. They describe themselves as 'a global corporate citizen with long traditions. . . . Since our inception in 1872 our company has been a vital part of many of the communities in which we operate'. In 2001 Cable & Wireless had a turnover of £8 billion and customers in 70 countries.[43]

This company has been part of the globalisation project for more than 100 years; indeed many would argue that it has been central to that project. It is legitimate and profitable, and donates substantially to community projects all over the world. A global corporate citizen?

Enron

When Enron went into receivership in December 2001 it was the biggest bankruptcy in US history. Enron says its 'business is to create value and opportunity for your business. . . . It's difficult to talk about Enron without using the word "innovative". . . . We believe in the benefits of open, competitive wholesale markets. . . . No wonder that *Fortune* surveys have named Enron the most innovative company in America year after year.'[44]

Enron is (was) a legitimate business with solid relationships with US and UK political parties. As utility suppliers of electricity and water, the company supplied two products vital to life on planet Earth. Nobody can live without water, and most of us cannot now live without electricity – don't fool yourself. A good corporate citizen? When did it lose this status?

Scott Bader Company Limited

Scott Bader is owned 'in common' by all who work in it. The company was given to its employees on Scott Bader's retirement in 1951. He defined four tasks for any company:

- The economic task: to secure orders for products that can be designed, made and serviced in such a manner as to make a profit.
- The technical task: to enable marketing to secure profitable orders by keeping them supplied with up-to-date product design.
- The social task: to provide members of the company with opportunities for satisfaction and development through participation in the working community.

- The political task: to encourage other men and women to change society by offering them an example by being economically healthy and socially responsible.

Scott Bader is a producer of polymers and composites and has 650 employees working in the United Kingdom, France, Sweden, South Africa, the United Arab Emirates, the Czech Republic and the United States. Its turnover was nearly £100 million in 1999.

Unilever

'[Unilever] always strives to be a trusted corporate citizen, fulfilling [their] responsibilities to the communities in which [they] operate.'[45] As I have noted elsewhere in this book, it is possible to live a Unilever life, rarely stepping outside the boundaries of that company's products. Don't you fancy a Magnum ice cream while you're reading this?

An Anglo-Dutch food, home and personal care conglomerate, this company prides itself on its sense of responsibility and has engaged not just in community investment but in supporting new corporate citizenship initiatives. But its sets its own standards and is like few other companies: it operates in 150 countries and had 150 million customers a day in 1999. It describes itself as 'a multi-local multinational company'.

A multi-local corporate citizen?

Spearmint Rhino

Spearmint Rhino is a US table dancing company.[46] After successfully launching in the United States in January 2002, they developed a strategy to establish some 100 clubs in the United Kingdom. The founder, John Cray, said that he expected there to be few problems. As he said: 'It's better for us (in the United Kingdom) than in the United States from the standpoint that your reputation counts. If you're a good corporate citizen, you're appreciated by the authorities. . . . Within five years we'll have 100 clubs with a combined turnover of $500 million.'[47]

Spearmint Rhino is a legitimate business, making money and observing all the rules. Many would claim that it provides entertainment, creates jobs and contributes to the well-being of the communities in which it operates. Is it a good corporate citizen?

British Airports Authority (BAA): an approach to corporate citizenship

Six key points – three key players

One:	Avoid cosmetic solutions.
Two:	Adopt a reasonable approach to pressure groups.
Three:	Leadership must come from the top . . . there are three key players:

- The Chief Executive
- Corporate & Public Affairs Director
- Community Relations or Social Responsibility Director.

Four:	It's not just about money.
Five:	Look for the synergies.
Six:	Communicate:

'There will come a day when it will seem extraordinary that there were ever companies that did not embrace corporate citizenship' (Mike Hodgkinson, CEO BAA plc).[48]

BAA runs most of the United Kingdom's airports.

In the case of Scott Bader and BAA we have two companies whose approaches to corporate citizenship are radically different. These two contrasting examples, 50 years apart but both still thriving companies, clearly address many of the management issues identified earlier, particularly when it comes to communications and stakeholder engagement.

The different perspectives on corporate citizenship can be collected under a few headings. These reflect both areas of interest for researchers and more public concerns.

- defining the boundaries of corporate activity
- controlling decision making
- the morality of individual and corporate decision making

- engaging with society through consultation and reporting
- contributing to the common good.

Corporate complicity and spheres of influence

Of the world's largest 100 economies, some 50 are companies, not countries.[49] Many of the largest companies straddle the world and are effectively supra-territorial bodies of no fixed abode. It is therefore not surprising that there has been increased interest in defining the boundaries of corporate activity and their role, scope, power and responsibilities. Unilever, as mentioned earlier, operates in some 150 countries with a range of products from fish to detergents. Its supply chains stretch around the world, and it sells to 150 million individuals everyday; its tentacles touch perhaps 10 per cent of the population of the world.[50] Apparently the company 'meets the everyday needs of people everywhere' by selling 500 million litres of ice cream every day![51]

In the struggle for personal identity and in the effort to gain some control or least understanding of the world around us, we move between the amorphous state and the physicality of our local communities while bouncing up against the brands of the global corporations. The economist and social philosopher John Galbraith in his 93rd year has said that these corporations are out of control; that they are beyond human intervention. These new entities 'have grown out of effective control by the owners, the stockholders, into nearly absolute control by the management and individuals recruited by management'. They are, he says, almost beyond monitoring.[52]

It is a useful exercise to take a map of the world and draw on it the domicility of *Fortune 500* companies. Then mark the countries in which they operate in some form or other, making sure to indicate the manner of the relationship with that country. It quickly becomes apparent that the dramatic increase in world trade has been brought about by, and has most benefited, some 500 companies trading within three trading blocks: Europe, North America and Japan/China/Southeast Asia.

The first two principles of the UN Global Compact and many of the emerging human rights guidelines are also concerned with the two issues of complicity in human rights abuses and the corporation's sphere of influence.[53] From another perspective the stewardship of supply chains also asks the same question: to what extent should or can a company be responsible for its contractors and suppliers? This question is also posed through the concept of ecological footprints, which is concerned with the total impact of a particular process, decision or product, taking into account all possible environmental implications.

The morality of individual and corporate decision making

There is an innate interest about other people who seem to be able to gain power and those who appear powerful. Normally this is also associated with being rich, when discussed in the context of business. When people are deemed to be powerful but poor there is the utmost respect. Wealth, power and a sense of responsibility are also a rare combination. In conversations with senior business executives most deny that they are powerful, or that their job demands that they reflect on the relationship between wealth, power and responsibility.

Yve Newbold was a long-serving member of the boards of Coutts Bank (where the British Royal Family do business: 'expert wealth management for private citizens'), the Hanson Corporation (from bricks to batteries to racehorses to being the model of Thatcher's economics) and BT (the winner of many awards for social and environmental reporting and engagement).[54] Writing in 2001 she said, 'people are surprised when I tell them that in 20 years in the boardroom not once do I recall a discussion on the moral or ethical implications of any decision made by the board'.[55] It was not, she said, 'that the people lacked an ethical framework of reference but that the language of the boardroom was finance'.

She said that communication by the companies was directed at:

- institutional shareholders;
- financial analysts;
- the financial press, and then
- the private shareholder.

She says: 'The principles of shareholder democracy did not extend to include others embraced within the newly fashionable but vague nomenclature of 'stakeholder', such as employees or society as a whole.'

Conversations with power (1)

The chairmen

As an example of research into attitudes to power, wealth and corporate social responsibility here is direct transcription of a conversation with the chairmen of two of the world's largest corporations:

Q: Why do you engage in stakeholder consultation, social and environmental auditing and reporting and public policy?
We only engage in this sort of activity because it is good business. To suggest that in the boardroom we are concerned with public policy is wrong. We are only interested in focusing our attention on the good of the business, on making sure that we can stay in business, in ensuring that we can reward investors and secure their long-term investment in our business.

Q: So, when you are making decisions for the company you are not making them for the public good?
Only in the sense that the company's good can be the public good.

Q: But in making decisions do you not think about the effect that they could have beyond the company's sphere of influence?
We understand that we have an effect, and we aim to be a good company – socially and environmentally responsible – but it is not our intention to be anything other than good businessmen.

Q: Do you have no moral compass by which to make business decisions? Do you not take your personal values into the boardroom?'
Yes, but only on behalf of the company and its survival.

Q: But if I said that your company is exemplary in many ways, and that by its behaviour it raises standards in some parts of the world – particularly in areas like health and safety and internal employment practices – what would you say?
Well it's nice of you to say so, but this really is not our intention.

Q: So what do you do with your power – with the fact that your actions are exemplary and that you could often be a force for good in society?

Being a good company, successfully rewarding shareholders is enough, and going about our business in a socially and environmentally responsible way is enough for us.

The chairman of another large international company interjects:

I do not believe that corporate directors lose their personal values when they enter the boardroom. We have moral compasses, and we must not deny this. The suggestions that, first, the company can operate without regard for society's values, and, second, that the company has a life beyond that of its directors, is not right. If the company director's values are the same as those of the efficient corporation then this tells us something about the values of this company director.

Q: Does it not matter that your corporate behaviour saves lives, that by acting responsibly you are bettering the lives of people that come into contact with your company – particularly in some parts of the world where there is illegitimate or abusive government?

I am not interested in saving lives; that is not our business. We must look after our employees' lives because that is good business – they are an important asset for us and without them we could not survive.

Reflecting on this I asked a large group of significant board members of some of the world's largest companies how they saw the situation.[56] The different discussions in varying locations took place over a period of 12 months, in large groups or individually. Initially they were outraged by the suggestion that their moral compasses were somehow deficient. As we discussed the situation the complexities and nuances of their directorial lives became clearer, and much anecdotal evidence came to light that supported Newbold's explanation that the language of the board room is generally concerned with financial values, not social value. These were the issues that arose:

- Many of them served on each other's boards.
- The vast majority were men.
- They were mostly over 50 years old.

- Apart from a few exceptions they were white.
- They felt a weight of responsibility, but it was towards the share price.
- They denied being able to feel wider responsibilities because they were servants of the corporation and the market: this is virtuous in itself, they argued.
- But they all felt the changing expectations of society and had stories to tell of how they had inspired significant changes in their companies' portfolios, personnel or working practices in order to counter outside attacks.
- They generally saw activist civil society organisations, particularly environmental and human rights NGOs, as 'an enemy of the market'. These people, they argued, did not understand either market processes or how decision making occurred in large private corporations.
- They admitted living very affluent and privileged lives, rarely having to encounter the daily degradations and frustrations of crowded public transport, hunger or a leaking roof. Indeed their contact with either the beneficiaries or the losers of their decision making was either mediated by someone else or, if it occurred at all, minimal.

The most striking revelation was the overall sense that they denied responsibility for issues beyond the company's financial status. This can be put down to two factors. First, time is tight and large corporations are extremely complex organisations; limiting boardroom discussion to financial performance makes for greater focus. Second, directors of publicly quoted corporations arrive at the top with a history of loyal service to the system that has created their personal wealth and power. If we think of the corporation as a tube of toothpaste, then these people are extruded or squeezed out of the top to become agents for the greater good of the company. As one of them said in a cry of anguish: 'You think we have responsibility, but we have less control over our decision making than middle ranking executives.'

Many years ago when researching Britain's biggest business, the arms industry, I was told by a very senior civil servant who had moved from the UK's Ministry of Defence (MOD) to a major engineering company that business was so much simpler and less stressful than the machinery of government. Here, he said in his new post on the board of the company, 'we just think about making money; in the MOD we had to deal with the complexities of balancing logistics, politics and policy'.[57] He was sure that

Conversations with power (2)

The bank

The man speaking is trying to face two ways at the same time. Inevitably he falls over his own words. It is 2002, a month after the Enron scandal. I am at a conference on governance in Europe. In front of me an investment analyst from the corporate affairs department of one of Europe's largest banks is making his presentation.

First he shows a slide that has the name of his bank proudly displayed; in the middle is a quote from the Secretary-General of the United Nations, Kofi Annan. It says: 'Globalisation is good for everyone etc.'

So he begins with the public good.

He ends by telling us the rationale for the bank's new foundation for Africa. 'This is a long term investment for us to leverage new market opportunities, to create more wealth for the Bank's shareholders. . . . This is philanthropy for future competitive advantage.'

He ends with private wealth.

At no point does he indicate the link between the creation, development and expansion of market activity in Africa and the possibility of delivering public goods. There is a link, but he doesn't make it. He wants to tell us how responsible his company is in being a good global corporate citizen, but he also wants to reassure his investors that they are being responsible capitalists. The point is that the only way this will work, without the analyst having to go down Alice's rabbit hole to Wonderland is by making the link; by explaining that his bank has a part to play in the establishment of markets *and* participatory politics *and* healthy civil society. One of the greatest impediments to peace in transitional societies is the failure of the corporate community to display a coherent sense of the structure of society, as opposed to the securing of private wealth.

his fellow directors, who had spent a lifetime immersed in business, would argue that they too had to manage complexity, but, he argued, at the end of the day all that mattered in business was money. At the end of the day in government what mattered was survival, public approval, international relations, and putting policy into practice. You could not sell up and get out. Voters could change allegiance and thereby change government, but the civil service was always left with the business of trying to run the country.

'Raising a ladder to the moon: after years of toil, and the application of all that energy, science, or money could procure, the problem has been solved'

It is certain that the originators of the Atlantic Cable, to whom is due the honour of being the pioneers of ocean telegraphy (when their scheme ranked in public opinion, only one degree in the scale of absurdity below that of raising a ladder to the moon) imagined the success would be rewarded by great and permanent remuneration.[58]

(Henry Moriarty, 7 March 1870, navigator on *The Great Eastern*, the ship that laid the first two trans-Atlantic telegraph cables, in a letter to the Editor of the London *Standard*)

The laying of the first telegraph cable from Europe to North America could provide the foundation for a heroic adventure film script full of portent, dilemmas and bravery. Raising the necessary investment for the first cable across the Atlantic was difficult enough, but when it broke after just four days raising more investment to repeat the experiment was fortitude personified, even though the first experiment had been a resounding success. Nation had spoken to nation, directly by telegraph for the first time and the human project was about to move on.

Henry Moriarty's letter is from the archives of Cable & Wireless in Porthcurno in Cornwall where the first trans-Atlantic cable came ashore. Having compared the connecting of two continents with a copper cable as not unlike 'raising a ladder to the moon', Moriarty goes on to complain about the fact that success breeds success. Now that it had been shown that it was possible to shrink distance by having virtually simultaneous communication between two great trading nations, he complains that other entrepreneurs are getting in on the act:

After years of toil, and the application of all that energy, science, or money could procure, the problem has been solved; the practicability of the once wild scheme so successfully demonstrated, that we are now led to believe that, every CheapJohn Company, which pleases to make another cable to lay at the side of it, is at liberty to do so.[59]

Cable & Wireless survived the twentieth century and into the twenty-first, riding the wave of changes in telecommunications and media that were at the heart of the twentieth century. Their success was due to several factors: being at the heart of the British Empire and thereby deriving benefit from being on the winning side, managing the growth of international business development, driving technological change, and continuing to be entrepreneurial pioneers. But also, perhaps more important than all these factors, although also because of them, was the individual character of the company and its leaders.

In 2002 Cable and Wireless divided into two entities. Cable & Wireless Global concentrates on the economic powerhouse regions of the world – Europe, North America and Japan – while Cable & Wireless Regional takes care of some of their most long-established markets in the Caribbean and Panama. Promising that 'we deliver the Internet promise', the company now operates in 80 countries, with 84 hubs around the world in 60 countries, with 48,000 km of fibre network and 460,000 km of submarine cable around the world: the second largest network in the world.

Cable & Wireless are symbolic of that which now governs our lives. They are globalisation personified. They manufacture nothing, but they handle our dreams, our chatter and our illusions. They have laid down their cables that we may connect.

Historian Eric Hobsbawm has said that the twentieth century was the century of technology and economics.[60] Others have commented that in terms of business the nineteenth century was the century of the entrepreneur, the twentieth the century of management and the twenty-first will be the century of governance.[61]

E. M. Forster pleaded in *A Passage To India* for East to meet West: 'Only connect,' he said. Now we can, as Ulrich Beck says, 'criss-cross and undermine sovereign national states . . . with varying prospects of power, orientation, identities and networks'.[62] Cable & Wireless are one company at the heart of the globalisation project and they give us globality: the ability to think and act with a global world-view as customers and consumers of space, time and materiality.[63]

In the early twenty-first century the concept of organisation is changing. As the guru of organisational metaphor, Gareth Morgan, says: 'The concept of organisation is a product of the mechanical age. Now that we are living in an electronic age, new organising principles are necessary.'[64]

The electronic age is also the global age where corporate domicility is a product of history – as with Nestlé's base in Switzerland – or convenience – as with Virgin's base in the Cayman Island – to avoid paying taxes. Both Nestlé and Virgin operate globally; both are trans-national and supra-territorial in the sense that they are not necessarily bound by local laws and customs – until they land. These companies are valued more for their brands than any other asset they may have acquired, financial, logistical or human.

Globalisation

There is an inevitability about the globalisation project, because it is largely driven by economics and trade made possible by communications technology. This is recognised by those, like Will Hutton, who wish to see the project facing up to social and environmental challenges as well as those who think that whatever happens is inevitable, like Thomas Friedman and John Micklethwait.[65] Hutton says: 'The attempt to isolate economics from other disciplines has fatally disabled its power to explain what is happening in the world.'[66] Micklethwait and Wooldridge are positive about the benefits of globalisation. 'The bulwarks of our defence (of globalisation) has been economic. . . . The simple fact is that globalisation makes us richer, or makes enough of us richer to make the whole project worthwhile.'[67] But there is little mention of the state of the natural environment or growing wealth inequality, or the fact that these two issues are creating not just local difficulties but global conflict.

In an effort to explain some of the complexities of globalisation, and to dispel some of the polarisation and inflamed passion that has taken place around the subject, Jan Aart Scholte has categorised five elements of globalisation: internationalisation; liberalisation; universalisation; Westernisation, modernisation or Americanisation; and deterritorialisation or supraterritoriality. This analysis is most helpful as it forces all those engaged in the debate for and against globalisation to re-categorise existing arguments. For example, let us take the ephemerality of a pop star such as Britney Spears. Which of Scholte's categories can be applied to this description of her in London's *Sunday Times* in 2002?

> She's global capitalism in a micro-mini. She's junk food. Britney is the triumph of America made flesh – one more time.[68]

Do we have all five categories in one body?

In essence Scholte supports the idea that we are now talking about social space as much as territory when we refer to globalisation. As he says: 'Globalisation is understood as transformation of social space marked by the growth of supraterritorial connections between people. This reconfiguration of geography has profound implications for governance. No longer can public affairs be managed through the territorialist framework of sovereign states.'[69]

In an effort to promote global values, and develop universalisation by putting some checks and balances on economic liberalisation, the UN Secretary-General in concert with colleagues developed and promoted the Global Compact in 1999. As he said, we have a choice: 'Let us choose to reconcile the creative forces of private entrepreneurship with the needs of the disadvantaged.'[70] This can be read as a new universalisation of the modernist project of liberalisation and development going hand in hand.

Deterritorialisation and supraterritoriality

New organisational forms linked to reputation and brand management have a direct bearing on corporate citizenship, and without an analysis of these features any discussion of accountability, governance or partnerships will tend towards confusion. If we begin with the premise that classical organisational forms are disintegrating, or that there are a multiplicity of organisational forms, then we can perhaps begin to unravel the relationship between human activity, the planet and people.

There is now a digression from hard boundaries of organisations to looser, more informal working arrangements between empowered knowledge workers. It applies to all organisations, across all sectors. [71] It is not post-industrial, in the sense that industrial workplace settings continue and range from thousands of workers sitting in serried ranks sewing GAP sweatshirts in Saipan to thousands of workers sitting in serried ranks in call centres in BT facilities in Glasgow. But marketing, research, development and management functions now operate on different principles.

To organise could now mean surfing between organisation as in: To organise – to move from one organisational culture to another. A bit like Saturday morning shopping, or surfing the net, or managing to pay bills on the net. Antidote: the Scottish Highlands, a desert island, inside your head. Old meaning: to get things into shape. Now it means to get shapes into things.

The development of network organisations as global phenomena is not limited to business. The growth of international non-government organi-sations (INGOs) is well documented.[72] Many INGOs with a media pres-ence may actually operate using a handful of individuals working on an informal, voluntary basis. Some NGOs draw funds from public and/or private sources, while others are founded on a substantial membership base. The introduction referred to the membership of NGOs such as Greenpeace International, Amnesty International and the RSPB.[73] Their accountability and governance structures span the entrepreneurial–institu-tional spectrum, with an increasing number demonstrating the resources and organisation of professional organisations.

NGOs are a diverse and heterogeneous group of organisations whose numbers have grown significantly in the last decade. Figures to describe this situation fully have yet to be produced with any accuracy, but the following statistics provide an indication of NGO growth.

- The Union of International Associations, which gathers global statistics on NGOs, in 1999 estimated that there were more than 50,000 international or transnational NGOs (INGOs).[74]
- Of these groups, well over 1000 have consultative status with the UN Economic and Social Council.[75]
- In England and Wales there were more than 186,248 registered 'non-governmental' charities at the end of 1998.[76]

The management challenge

The best-selling books by global management gurus all tell the same story about the challenges faced by workers and managers. As all gurus are vision-ary, they all talk of a paradigm shift. Thomas Kuhn, the originator of the expression, would shift in his grave! One of the management gurus with the greatest longevity is Peter Drucker. He has concluded, after some 60 years of cogitation, that 'the center of a modern society, economy and community is not technology. It is not information. It is not productivity. It is the managed institution as the organ of society to produce results.' Drucker's paradigm shift is in arguing that 'management's concern and management's responsi-bility are everything that affects the performance of the institution and its results – whether inside or outside, whether under the institution's control or totally beyond it'. His revised list of concerns is now: management, respon-sibility, performance, strategy, change, information, knowledge-workers and personnel management.[77]

In this last category he is echoed by Stephen Covey, whose seven habits for highly effective people are: 'be proactive, begin with the end in mind, put first things first, think win–win, seek first to understand then to be under-stood, synergize, and sharpen the saw'.[78] I presume that these would apply to CEOs, mothers, teachers, politicians, soccer managers and the leaders of orchestras. These are also principles that are at the heart of corporate citi-zenship. For instance companies are encouraged to think of their total impact on society, which requires upstream and downstream thinking ('the end in mind'), to consult with and report to a range of stakeholders ('understand then be understood') and find common ground ('synergize').

Other guides to the management agenda include: leadership and no-leadership, change, information to knowledge, value and values, creativity and innovation, workplace networking, organising and organisations. In 'Management 21C' Subir Chowdhury argues that 'the twenty-first century leader's most valuable asset will be the ability to dream'.[79] In this Chowd-hury, Covey and Drucker mirror two of the most radical thinkers on corpo-rate citizenship, Ernest Bader (*The Man Who Gave His Company Away*), and E. F. Schumacher, author of *Small Is Beautiful*, who deliberated on the evolution of organisations as 'a learning process'.[80]

Many of the management 'gods' have written that this is a time of change, or great change, or unending change, or permanent change or uncertainty.

Among them are Peter Senge and his colleagues based loosely at the Massachusetts Institute of Technology, who, writing in 1999, ask: 'Does anyone expect the next 20 years to be less tumultuous than the last 20 years? Given the changes expected in technology, biology, medicine, social values, demography, the environment, and international relations, what kind of world might humanity face?' These are reasonable questions, given that this team is concerned with making our organisations and enterprises more

---

Hot air: management and engineering

This story was doing the rounds on the net in December 2001. If you have reached a position of any power or responsibility, please ponder, and I apologise to the original author; on the net everything is everyone's:

A man in a hot air balloon realised he was lost. He reduced altitude and spotted a man below. He descended a bit more and shouted, 'Excuse me, can you help? I promised a friend I would meet him an hour ago, but I don't know where I am!'

The man below replied, 'You are in a hot air balloon hovering approx. 30 feet above the ground. You are between 49 and 51 degrees north latitude and between 120 and 125 degrees west longitude.'

'You must be an engineer,' said the balloonist.

'I am,' replied the man on the ground, 'How did you know?'

'Well,' answered the balloonist, 'everything you told me is technically correct, but I have no idea what to make of your information and the fact is, I am still lost. Frankly, you've not been much help so far.'

The man below responded, 'You must be in management.'

'I am' replied the balloonist, 'but how did you know?'

'Well,' said the man on the ground, 'you don't know where you are or where you are going. You have risen to where you are due to a large quantity of hot air. You made a promise you have no idea how to keep, and you expect people beneath you to solve your problems. The fact is you are exactly in the same position you were in before we met, but now, somehow, it's my fault.'

adaptive to changing external and internal environments. Their task is to map the fundamentals of organisational change, but, as they say, 'for most of human history intrepid explorers have set out on their journeys of discovery without comprehensive maps'.[81] This may have some truth; they may not have had clear maps but they often had clear visions of the meaning of life and of their purpose as humans on Earth.

Economics and globalisation

In the world of corporate citizenship there is a trend towards global social and environmental standards and management systems. These are designed to complement the post-Bretton Woods global financial and trade mechanisms now embedded in the World Trade Organisation. For some commentators economics is the entry point to corporate citizenship. This is accountant and academic Richard Whitley:

> Since a number of quite distinct forms of economic organisation have developed and continue to be reproduced as separate variants of industrial capitalism since the early nineteenth century, I suggest that it would be more productive to understand the processes underlying such divergences.[82]

In moves to solve the problem posed by Samuel P. Huntingdon's *Clash of Civilisations*, the world is increasingly adopting compacts, initiatives and conventions based on universal human rights treaties that have been agreed by nation-states since 1945.[83] Perhaps the most significant is the 1948 Universal Declaration on Human Rights. At the global supraterritorial level, these moves have great appeal to a small group of multinational corporations and international institutions alike because they provide frameworks for legitimising their activities.

There are two problems with this simplistic approach. First, there is a general ignorance of the standards and a lack of implementation at the local level, particularly in developing countries. Second, a rights- and values-based approach to life is antithetical to a significant proportion of business enterprises. From the global arms and drugs trader to the international retailer to the smallest of street-side enterprises, the primary desire is to engage in commerce that provides a good return on capital and effort, *not* to aid the common good.

Eight of the most prominent global corporate citizenship initiatives in 2003 are:

- The UN Global Compact
- ILO Conventions
- The OECD Guidelines for Multinational Enterprises
- ISO 14000 Series
- AccountAbility 1000
- The Global Reporting Initiative
- The Global Sullivan Principles
- Social Accountability 8000.[84]

These initiatives are attempts to address the dilemma posed by George Soros, among others, who says in his 1998 *The Crisis of Global Capitalism*:

> I consider the failures of politics much more pervasive and debilitating than the failures of the market mechanism. Individual decision making as expressed through the market mechanism is much more effective than collective decision making as practised in the international arena.[85]

The corporate citizenship initiatives referred to here have three components. First, they derive their legitimacy from nation-states as actors; second, they have to be implemented at the local community level; and third, they gain their momentum from global organisations that are supra-territorial.

One of the driving forces of politics, local and global, in the twenty-first century is the commonality of chatter. The Swiss constitution has for a long time called on citizens to vote regularly on issues, as well as for politicians. Elsewhere in the world, particularly in social democracies, there has been an explosion of focus groups, stakeholder consultations and instant voting for all manner of things from 'Who is more beautiful: Posh Spice or Madonna?' to 'Should the United States drop a nuclear bomb on Afghanistan/ Iraq/ North Korea?'

There is an extended electronic neural network that never sleeps and steals all our time.

'What is this life if there is no time to stand and stare?'

Corporate citizenship in action (1): McAfrika

This story is about Africa, and particularly South Africa, but it is global too. The question is: does Africa need McDonald's more than McDonald's needs Africa? This story was inspired by reading in the global news media – an electronic newsletter – of the launch in the Norwegian capital, Oslo, of a new product: the McAfrika sandwich. I was in South Africa at the time talking to NGOs, businesses, government officials and others about development, sustainability and corporate citizenship.

What some would see as the savagery of McDonald's insensitivity to development issues and poverty is in direct contrast with an inspiring speech made by South Africa's President Thabo Mbeki on the occasion of the unveiling of South Africa's new constitution. The constitution is an innovative, inspiring document that includes reference to sustainability, child labour and peace making.

> The McAfrika sandwich will be sold as part of a rotating exotic food series in Norway, which has 60 McDonald's restaurants.
>
> (*Washington Times*, 27 August 2002)

> We are committed to making the world a better place and to providing socially responsible leadership in every community where we do business. We are committed to greater transparency, continuous improvement, and dialogue on the issues.
>
> (McDonald's.com, December 2002)

I am an African.

I owe my being to the hills and the valleys, the mountains and the glades, the rivers, the deserts, the trees, the flowers, the seas and the ever-changing seasons that define the face of our native land.

My body has frozen in our frosts and in our latter day snows. It has thawed in the warmth of our sunshine and melted in the heat of the midday sun. The crack and the rumble of the summer thunders, lashed by startling lightening, have been causes both of trembling and of hope.

The fragrances of nature have been as pleasant to us as the sight of the wild blooms of the citizens of the veldt. The dramatic shapes of the Drakensberg, the soil-coloured waters of the Lekoa, iGqili noThukela, and the sands of the Kgalagadi, have all been panels of the set on the natural stage on which we act out the foolish deeds of the theatre of our day.

At times, and in fear, I have wondered whether I should concede equal citizenship of our country to the leopard and the lion, the elephant and the springbok, the hyena, the black mamba and the pestilential mosquito. A human presence among all these, a feature on the face of our native land thus defined, I know that none dare challenge me when I say – I am an African!

I owe my being to the Khoi and the San whose desolate souls haunt the great expanses of the beautiful Cape – they who fell victim to the most merciless genocide our native land has ever seen, they who were the first to lose their lives in the struggle to defend our freedom and dependence and they who, as a people, perished in the result.

Today, as a country, we keep an audible silence about these ancestors of the generations that live, fearful to admit the horror of a former deed, seeking to obliterate from our memories a cruel occurrence which, in its remembering, should teach us not and never to be inhuman again.'

(South African President Thabo Mbeki, November 1996)[86]

As I drive out of Cape Town, on the left of the superhighway are the gleaming sparkles of the new shopping mall, and on the right are the tin shacks of the township. This is South Africa in 2002; this is a country struggling to measure its success after eight years of the democratic alternative to apartheid. And yet apartheid in the form of wealth division is every where. In 2003 33 per cent of the population survive in a cycle of poverty and powerlessness.[87] As one black activist put it: 'The whites made sure that they had the best infrastructure. And they still have.' Although, as he pointed out, the new social mobility means that there is an emerging black middle class and there are now poor white families living in previously all-black townships.

In the days before the Johannesburg world summit on sustainable development with its themes of 'people, planet and prosperity', McDonald's in Norway launches a new sandwich called the McAfrika, composed of layers of beef, cheese, tomatoes and salad in pitta bread. The new product costs £2.80 or SA Rand 42: enough to keep death from the door in Africa for a week. McDonald's may be a global corporation and have produced its first social report in 2002, but this does not mean that McDonald's Norway has much sensitivity to the 12 million people near starvation in sub-Saharan Africa or the 15 million people who just survive in South Africa. McDonald's refused to withdraw the McAfrika despite protestations from Norwegian Church Aid who said: 'It's inappropriate and distasteful to launch a hamburger called McAfrika when portions of southern Africa are on the verge of starvation.' Their restaurants were also picketed by protesters distributing starvation crackers to potential customers.[88]

McDonald's strategy is to turn the Big Mac into a global brand to rival Coca-Cola. The group opened its 30,000th restaurant worldwide in 2002 and has franchises in more than 120 countries. It served more than 46 million customers every day in 2001; that's nearly 16.8 billion servings a year. On any day it serves 0.1 per cent of the world population, which as the company says, leaves plenty of room for growth.[89] In South Africa McDonald's opened its restaurant in 1996 in Johannesburg, having won a significant legal ruling claiming South African recognition of their global trade marks: the name and the golden arches. The global–local dimension was present in their decision to pursue what they considered to be their intellectual property. One of the South African government's reasons for supporting McDonald's in this case was their bid at the time (1996) to host the 2004 Olympic Games. To be successful the Games would need sponsorship from global corporations. Those corporations in turn needed to be reassured that their profits and property would be protected by the state.

A savage irony for South Africa is that it has similar obesity statistics to the United States. Some 60 per cent of US citizens are classified as obese, and so are 60 per cent of women and 40 per cent of men in South Africa. In both cases, it can be argued, the issues are ignorance of diet, low educational attainment and lack of access to nourishing, healthy, readily available, affordable foods. There is also the issue of seduction and corruption.

After all, McDonald's sells both food and lifestyle. Its foods also contain significant levels of sugar and saturated fat. But this is not one international comparator that either South African or US citizens would have expected. The public policy issue in South Africa, and in the United States, is who should take responsibility? As the South African economy grows, the spending power of all its citizens will mean that they are tempted by cheap fast food. This has already happened in the townships where 3.5 million households were connected to the electricity grid between 1994 and 2002, resulting in a boom in electronic goods. Some 80 per cent of South African households now have TV.

Much has been written about the 'McDonaldisation' of the planet but here we see a clear case where Scholte's five categories of globalisation can be applied.[90] There is no doubt that this international company represents the global homogenisation of food and the Westernisation of lifestyles. It also desires the liberalisation of the South African economy to allow it to invest. Most importantly it raises the identity of the individual consumer to a point beyond being South African by connections with another world of global citizenship based on consumption patterns and dreams of modernity. In a world of turmoil McDonald's, like Disney and Coke, represents a simple, clarified world where full stomachs and instant gratification are guaranteed. This social space concerns the supraterritoriality of the globalisation process. Scholte has talked about 'the respacialisation of social relations' through the 'supraterritoral connections between people'. Here we see McDonald's desire to follow an economic growth path to feed more than 0.1 per cent of the global population, with countries such as South Africa firmly in their sights. But for what reason, other than power and profitability? Doesn't 0.1 per cent already represent a monopolistic position?

Post-apartheid South Africa could epitomise the 'single bottom line' approach of *A Ladder to the Moon*. There is a democratically elected government, a vibrant market economy, and a highly developed civil society sector. This model of social democracy has its South African characteristics. The ANC is the party in power with members of rival parties in the cabinet, and at present the ANC dominates the political scene making the proposition of an alternative government at present a chimera. But the robust new constitution contains checks and balances that make the situation in the United Kingdom, for instance, look feudal by comparison. The rule of law, when it can be enforced, is firmly entrenched in South African life.

The market has extremes. In the townships the air is full of the smell of cooking meat, mostly pork, bought and sold without regard for any of the country's health and safety laws. This meat, alongside fruit and vegetables, forms of the basis of the South African subsistence diet in the most impoverished townships. This is supplemented by large doses of *ganja* and alcohol. This is the underground or informal economy, which is estimated to account for 15 per cent of South Africa's GDP and employs three million people.[91] It is to this market that McDonald's hopes to bring fast food, developing a service economy and bringing health and safety awareness levels on the way as it has done in other emerging economies in the past. For instance in Moscow in the 1980s it raised food and animal health standards, in the United States in the 1990s it promoted traceability of all its meat products so that it could prove that its meat was BSE free and not derived from a rainforest area of the world. It is one of the first global fast food chains to produce a social report that is respectable enough to contain statements from Conservation International, Environmental Defense, the Natural Step and Business for Social Responsibility.[92]

At the other end of the spectrum South Africa is host to some of the world's largest multi-national corporations, most notably Anglo American, which seems to pervade every level of life in the same way as the ANC. Their aim is: 'To provide superior returns to our shareholders' as well as 'shouldering our share of social and environmental responsibilities as complementary'.[93] A sort of shareholder value with the burden of the planet and people as well. In 2002 it was announced that their next Chairman is to be Mark Moody-Stuart, formerly Chairman of Royal Dutch/Shell who are leaders in social and environmental reporting. The company refers to 'good citizenship' being a universal principle throughout all the company's operations in 40 countries. They say: 'We need to show that we use our resources and influence in society to the good' and that 'sustainable development is about conducting business with an eye to the needs of the future' – theirs and the societies in which they operate, presumably.

Recognising the delicate balance, but separation of the state and society the company says: 'The primary responsibility for the protection of human rights lies with governments and international organisations' but 'where it is within our power to do so, we will seek to promote the observation of human rights in the countries where we operate'. Clem Sunter, who in 2003 had been with Anglo American for 37 years, says in *Beyond Reasonable*

Greed, co-authored with Wayne Visser from KPMG: 'Bluntly put, we are seeking a reformation in business along the same lines as the one precipitated by Martin Luther in 1517.' Just as the excesses of the church and its indulgences led Luther to reject the church he had been brought up in, so too corporations have lost the confidence of their wider stakeholder groups. Given the fine rhetoric quoted above of Anglo American's commitment to sustainability and human rights, it is pertinent to quote Sunter and Visser:

> The modern equivalent of the flowery and unintelligible prayers which the Church used to recite in order to extract its indulgences from the peasantry is the purple prose and lofty sentiments expressed by companies in their mission statements.[94]

According to authoritative research by Mark Swilling from the new Sustainability Institute in Stellenbosch, just outside Cape Town, the size and scope of South Africa's civil society is significant. 'South Africa's civil society is as large in proportional terms and as vibrant as in all but a handful of advanced industrial countries.'[95] Civil society, in the guise of NGOs, is expected 'to act as monitors of the public good and safeguard the interests of the disadvantaged of society' as civil society 'represents the bridge between the citizenry, the state and the market'.[96] There are nearly 100,000 non-profit organisations in South Africa, the majority of which are informal community-based networks, often focused around health and HIV/AIDS issues. Many businesses see AIDS as the biggest single threat facing the country.[97] In the period 2002–7 it is estimated that half a million people will die of AIDS-related diseases, leaving behind some two million orphans.

There are, of course, other issues facing the country, such as providing basic services in clean water, electricity and health care. Most importantly there is the redistribution of wealth from the fantastically rich, predominantly white, sector of society to the poorest. This can be achieved by the state building houses and connecting services alongside the development of a skilled and educated workforce whose members both understand the past better and face the challenges of the future. The model of tri-sector development between the state, corporations and communities is currently balanced in favour of corporations so that they do not flee the country. The government tries desperately to provide the most basic services for the poorest communities while trying to keep global investors and affluent whites happy.

Surely some of the models of reconstruction from other countries that have suffered extreme oppression are relevant in South Africa today? What about ideas and inspiration from post-1945 Germany and Japan, post 1989-Eastern Europe, and the Philippines. The difference, as one long-standing social activist in South Africa observed, is that in Japan and Germany when citizens started to make money they reinvested in their own countries. In South Africa there is a tendency for the white community, particularly those closest to Britain, to reinvest outside South Africa. This means that, until there is an identifiably affluent South African investment class, the onus is on companies such as Anglo American and Old Mutual, who operate globally but have significant South African roots, to invest heavily in the development of civil and corporate governance and education among those who truly believe in South Africa. This will give substance to 'the purple prose and lofty sentiments of their mission statements'.[98]

South Africa abounds with wildlife. Ostriches stride speedily across the landscape and they make good eating, being similar to beef, so we can expect McOstrich and McWorld now that we have McAfrika!

Corporate citizenship in action (2): Unilever winning hearts and minds

The first World Detergent Congress (Paris, September 1954) had the effect of authorising the world to yield to Omo euphoria. . . . Advertisements for Omo involve the customer in a direct experience of the substance, making him the accomplice of a liberation rather than the mere beneficiary of the result; matter here is endowed with value-bearing states. [This] euphoria must not make us forget that there is one plane on which Persil and Omo are one and the same: the plane of the Anglo-Dutch trust Unilever.

(Roland Barthes)[99]

As the world market today is realized ever more completely, it tends to deconstruct the boundaries of the nation-state. . . . In the world market they appear increasingly as mere obstacles. . . . The ideology of the world market has always been the anti-foundational and anti-essentialist discourse par excellence. Circulation. mobility, diversity, and mixture are its possibility.

(Michael Hardt and Antonio Negri)[100]

Half of the world's 500 largest economies are corporations answerable only to themselves and effectively stateless, we have to rely on their own internal values to keep them honest and decent. . . .Today the skyscrapers of business tower over the old cathedrals. We must hope that those who build the enterprises within them are cathedral builders in their turn, for if they fail us we all fail.

(Charles Handy)[101]

Unilever's mission is meeting the everyday needs of people every-where. . . . Magnum (ice cream) is positioned as the essence of the pursuit of personal indulgence.

(unilever.com)

Dove soap helps Unilever clean up.

Profits up a third. Dove sales surged 60 per cent in Europe. But over-all sales growth only up 2 per cent. Overall profits up 35 per cent.

Continuing expansion in underlying margin reflects our determination to grow our business profitably.

(CEO, Niall Fitzgerald)

Ben & Jerry's ice cream strong sales in North America, UK sales of Hellmann's and Knorr products well up. 'Severely reduced consumer demand' in Argentina.

(26 April 2002 BBC News)[102]

From ice cream to soap, from Argentina to the United Kingdom, Unilever bestrides the planet unlike any nation-state. No wonder it calls itself a 'multi-local' multinational.

There are three reasons for choosing Unilever as an example here. First, its products are ubiquitous; they are part of my life and I suspect part of your life somewhere. Second, this is a company that has been proactive in its approach to corporate citizenship issues and it has stories to tell that can be described as best or better practice. Third, it iterates at all levels the dichotomy of aspiring to act, in its own words, 'legally, decently and honestly' while also arguing fervently for the self-regulation of business. Is it possible to detect, in articulating these two positions, the arrogance of size, affluence and overweening power, or is the company in fact articulating the politics of the possible? Apart from the excellence of some of their social and environmental reporting, how is it possible to get a handle on their governance, to know how they make decisions? How do those in power see the world?

Because of its diversity, its 'multi-local' stance and its trans-national nature it is the perfect example of Hardt and Negri's description of the world market as it now is. Again, despite its long history and the centrality of some of its products to some of our lives, it is barely referenced by name in most of the thick volumes reviewing the twentieth century. Another good reason for looking at Unilever is because it is *not* Nike, Royal/Dutch Shell, Nestlé or The Gap. It has not received high profile media attention for some alleged transgression of environmental, labour or human rights indiscretion.

By using a company such as Unilever we can also start in several different places to deconstruct the complexity of the company and see how it is part of the biopolitics of the world. Understanding it, as a trans-national corporation, is central to the management of the planet in the twenty-first

---

A Unilever life: peas and Ponds

With the Dove cradled not to drop it in her hand the water ran rivulets down her body as the day's stress washed away never had life been such a challenge as now that she had been given the task of handling Magnum as it broke new markets and soared above all other ice creams to the #1 spot as she dried herself carefully then to rub some Ponds in and look forward to a Birds Eye burger with Findus garden peas with just a little Hellmann's on the side before a quick burst of Impulse to meet her man in Axe . . . . her clothes were washed in Omo and her floors cleaned with Cif.

She was a woman about the planet.

This short story is *not* from Unilever.com

century. It bestrides the Earth with it products and its operations, with its sourcing and its distribution, with its employment, with its social systems, and with its governance. It is fascinating in its visibility and its invisibility. In the twenty-first century the analysis of such a company may be more revealing than looking at nation-states with their territoriality, politics, practices and legitimacy issues.

So how does *Unilever* derive its legitimacy? Why does it exist? Why can it continue? Charles Handy wrote that our great business institutions should be built like cathedrals because, unlike us mere mortals, some corporations seem to have immortality.

One way of understanding this company would be to look at it as an investor, or from a governance perspective. In 2000 this company had a turnover of 48.2 billion, employed 295,000 people worldwide, sold products in 150 countries, sold to 150 million people daily and handled a million electronic messages a day.

Another avenue would be to start with its products, which much of the world knows and loves: Magnum ice cream, Dove soap, Hellmann's mayonnaise, Knorr soups, Lipton's tea, Omo detergent, Birds Eye frozen fish, Axe/Lynx/Ego deodorant.

Unilever was formed in 1930 from the union of a British company, Lever Brothers, and a Dutch company, Margarine Unie, both dealing in palm oil to make soap and margarine. Its origins date back to 1885 and the marketing of Sunlight soap. Now the company sources some 7 per cent of the world's palm oil.

And here is Unilever selling one of its deodorants in 2002:

A stylish brand, Axe boosts young men's confidence and attraction through the combination of a distinctive masculine fragrance and long-lasting deodorant protection. Known as Lynx in the United Kingdom, Ireland, Australia and New Zealand and as Ego in South Africa, Axe is a range of male grooming toiletries including deodorant body spray, aftershave and shower gel products. Axe was launched as a perfumed body spray in France in 1983 and is now the number one male toiletries brand, available in 53 countries and dominant in Europe, South America and Australia. Recent innovations include modern fragrances; stylish packaging; and refreshing, revitalising aftershave lotions and shower gels.

A Unilever life: CEO Niall Fitzgerald

Just imagine how the story would read if it was integrated in the style of a cheap romantic novel – it might win hearts and minds:

'Ego-wearing Niall Fitzgerald, Chairman of Unilever plc, sank his teeth into the soft lusciousness of a Magnum as he spoke from the heart about the desperate need for clean water for all humankind. He smelt good that morning, having Axed himself down with the company's new revitalising shower gel as he stood under the cascades of clean, hot water. As he washed he ran through his speech: 'The basic challenge of sustainable agriculture is clear . . . we need to learn from the past . . . and we need to consider some of the applications of modern crop biotechnology.' As he had prepared for his big speech at Dublin Castle on 'whose future is it anyway' he confirmed the paramountcy of marketing above all else: 'it will be the consumer who shapes the future'.[103]

This short story is *not* from Unilever.com

So Unilever gives us science, sensibility, sexuality, love, responsibility and humour (one can only presume that this deodorant is called Ego in South Africa, and Axe and Lynx elsewhere in the world because someone at Unilever has a sense of humour!).

The boundaries of corporate activity and the sphere of influence

The company describes itself as 'multi-local', operates in 100 countries and sells its products in a total of 150 countries. The statistics are necessarily both fascinating and perhaps misleading. For instance they report that 177 billion cups of their tea are brewed every year and 150 million people buy their products daily.

In the language of the UN Global Compact, of which they are a supporter, their primary 'sphere of influence' is *either* specifically all the countries in which they have operations *or* also all those countries in which they sell or from which they source. Their secondary 'sphere of influence' is, without exaggeration, almost everyone on the planet through their sourcing, distribution and logistics, site operations, sales and governance. This means that they are among the most global of institutions and, with their range of products from hair care, to basic sanitation to essential foodstuffs, they are at the centre of the biopolitical structuring of planet Earth. Given that they source 90 per cent of their managers locally, the wonder is that they manage to maintain their global governance and control with such a small number of non-local managers.

Governance and the control of decision making

The governance of Unilever is based in the United Kingdom and the Netherlands. There are two companies, but with the same boards, missions and executives. (They are at pains to tell you that 'we are not like Shell' when it comes to corporate accountability and governance, but in reality the corporate culture of the company is not dissimilar, albeit operating with vegetable rather than fossil fuel oil.) While there is significant devolution of power and control to local units the main global boards, which have real control over local operations, are predominantly white, European men. The bulk of Unilever's customers are non-European, female and non-white. The corporate culture is based on European values of social cohesion, inclusivity and social democracy. They understand that their capitalism must uphold the rule of law, support participatory democracy and civil society fora, and that as a company they are accountability to Dutch and UK society.

The morality of individual and corporate decision making

As suggested in the previous section Unilever uphold democratic values and the rule of law. They go to great lengths on their website to explain their position on social responsibility issues, but this is based on an essential dichotomy. They hold positions that at first sight seem contradictory. In accordance with the UK's Advertising Standards Authority guidelines they comply with the dictum that their advertisements should be 'legal, decent and honest', while arguing fervently against further regulations on business activity globally. As a strong, self-assured company they have few fears about competition, believing that their products can stand the test of consumer choice. The paradoxical question that arises has to be: in the case of a global company with as many tentacles as Unilever, 'deconstructing the boundaries of the nation-state', how can we be sure that 'their own internal values keep them honest and decent'?[104]

Engaging with society through consultation and reporting

Unilever supports the OECD guidelines for multi-national enterprises, the UN Global Compact and the Global Sullivan Principles. At a local level they consult and report widely on a range of projects that are available through their website. But they have not referenced or apparently used such new corporate citizenship and accountability initiatives as the Global Reporting Initiative, AA1000S or SA8000. Like their compatriot Royal Dutch/Shell, with whom they compare themselves, they have close contact with all parts of their supply chain, from growers to distributors to end-users. But, unlike oil companies, they operate in some extremely competitive markets: ice cream and shampoo for instance. One thing is clear about this company: it does not want to be forced to have regulated conversations with its stakeholders. It will decide who they are and how it will report to them. It lists it stakeholders as investors, customers, suppliers and community and society and it divides its operations into two divisions: foods, and home and personal care.

Contributing to the common good

The ultimate challenge has been addressed by Unilever, they think. If it is believed that carrying palm oil round the world and adding value to it through mixing it with sweet-smelling aromas is intrinsically wrong because the price the consumer pays fails to incorporate a range of externalities, then Unilever is an evil entity. In this view of the world, its products destroy local culture and livelihoods, consume fossil fuel reserves and pollute the planet. If you believe that trade of this sort is wrong per se, then Unilever is a problem. If however Unilever is seen as a primary global neural network along whose lines move products, aspirations, dreams and lives then the vision may be different. It does not, as far as we know, launder money or deal in heroin or nuclear materials. It says it does not condone any form of child labour, but does not ascribe to any form of independent monitoring, although its social and environmental reports are 'verified' by an independent party.

Unilever's reputation is based on its products. It has also been proactive in its engagement with social partnership initiatives such as the Marine Stewardship Council. Through this initiative it aims to source all of its fish from 'certified, sustainable sources' by 2005. It has rarely been the target of high profile civil society protest. In one sense it is part of the old economy, as it buys raw materials and turns them into sophisticated products for a variety of markets in the developed and developing world. It uses the new economy to do business, apparently handling up to a million electronic messages a day. It has its own electronic neural network, the Unilever

---

A corrupting influence?

Michael Brockbank, Unilever Brand Communication vice president, conference on sponsorship in Chicago, 12 March 2002:

'Flora is the leading brand of margarine in the UK, used by all the family. The product formulation allows us to make heart health claims for it in other countries. In the UK we are severely restricted in health claims we can make in advertising. . . . Title sponsorship of the London Marathon, one of the world's biggest sport events in terms of participation, has been hugely beneficial to the brand. . . . Coverage of the event gets great attention, is strongly branded and communicates the brand's healthy benefits. The clip you saw was from a prime time television summary shown by the BBC in addition to their live coverage of the event during the day. *To get that amount of branded coverage on a channel which is not allowed to carry advertising is a major achievement.* . . . Last year's most famous sporting Brit, Sir Steven Redgrave and his wife were guest runners. Have a look at how we took this element of the sponsorship programme and made it the main theme of the advertising campaign, not just in print, but also on television.'[105]

intranet, as have all large organisations that bypass territory, time and distance.

On specific issues, it is quite clear that the world is there to be captured. For instance, because it sells quick and instant foods it is delighted that 33 per cent of meals bought in Europe are now fast foods, and that for the United States this figure is 50 per cent. It is delighted to work hard to circumnavigate various social controls, boasting for instance that by sponsoring both the London Marathon with Flora margarine and motor racing events it regularly manages to get television advertising on the BBC, which otherwise does not carry advertising. So, in this sense it operates to the current model of capitalism: to reward it investors with a growing rate of return, and to do this it must be competitive and invest in growth. How many more cups of tea does it want to have a bag in?

In the final analysis Unilever has a good record in keeping in touch with European and North American social concerns and in keeping close to its customers globally. In our current model it perhaps personifies 'good capitalism'. But it may be a model that requires some amendment. What, for instance, would happen to a company like Unilever if all its product prices were adjusted to include more social and environmental externalities? What would happen if the company had to report on comparable reporting standards across its financial, social and environmental performance? The answer is that we do not know; but we do know that it is companies like Unilever that operate alongside the Enrons and Worldcoms as well as alongside the world's biggest businesses in illegal drugs, sex, slavery and armaments.

Taking some responsibility for the new global governance is the next step to becoming a grown-up company. Adolescents have to grow up to take civic responsibility, to build cathedrals of the highest hopes and aspirations. Not just Magnums. If 'Unilever's mission is meeting the everyday needs of people everywhere', then there is more to life than 'the pursuit of personal indulgence'. Pass me a Magnum and some dignity and human rights, please. In the face of the evil that other companies and some governments do, Unilever has a responsibility to stand up taller in its pursuit of excellence, outstanding personal performance and responsible corporate citizenship. It cannot argue that it is one player on a crowded field doing its best to make the world a better place. It does make the world a better place: but if it does it must hold up the sword of truth.

Excerpts from Unilever's website

We have more experience in brand communication than any other company. We have more than 100 years of accumulated knowledge and we invest over £2 billion in our advertising campaigns every year. But there is no magic formula that will enable our brands to win the hearts and minds of consumers. Each advertising campaign is unique. On the way to work, in town or at home, consumers come across advertisements for our brands in all areas of their daily lives – on television, radio and the Internet, in print, posters and direct mail and through sponsorship and public relations campaigns.

Unilever's advertisement for Gibbs SR toothpaste, broadcast in 1955, was the very first television commercial produced in the United Kingdom. Since those early days, we have seen an explosion of the use of television as an advertising medium.

We are integrated into local economies and active in the communities where we operate. By the nature of our products, we play an important role in the daily lives of our consumers, providing them with brands that meet their everyday needs. We are part of society and aspire to be good corporate citizens in everything we do.

Unilever's five-year £1.25 million sponsorship agreement with London's Tate Modern enables the gallery to commission a new large-scale work for the Turbine Hall each year until 2004. Throughout the sponsorship period, The Unilever Series offers some of the world's leading artists the opportunity to unleash their creativity within this exciting space.

Louise Bourgeois created the inaugural work for The Unilever Series in 2000, with a sculpture entitled *Maman* – a giant spider, stood on the bridge over the Turbine Hall, and a set of three towers. They were seen by some three million visitors to the gallery.[106]

In the year 2002, at any one time, one billion people, or 16.6 per cent of the population, are using a Unilever product.

In 1967 John Lennon was criticised as blasphemous when he declared that the Beatles were more famous than Jesus Christ. But now some consumer products transcend religions in their reach into daily lives. How would the African concept of *Ubuntu* (humanity) sell if two billion dollars were spent on promoting it every year? If the combined advertising budgets of Unilever, Proctor and Gamble and AOL were spent on clean water we could solve the problem outlined by Margaret Thatcher's former environment minister, EU Commissioner Chris Patten (see the following chapter on sustainability).

I know, I know – c'mon get real, dear author – that's not how the world works.

It does not take a Ph.D. in politics, philosophy and economics to see the small adjustments that are needed to bring about radical changes in humanity on the planet.

Annual EU ice cream sales: 11 billion. Cost of providing clean water and sanitation to a billion people worldwide: $3.5 billion. Number of purchases of Unilever products annually: 365 billion. Amount Unilever spends on marketing annually: $2 billion. Revenues from private water sales (*excluding* bottled water) annually $300 billion.[107]

It's not just up to Unilever and corporate friends but governments and civil society too. You do get the feeling that with one great push we could this century achieve a better life for all on this planet. We aren't talking paradigm shift, rocket science or major brain surgery, but we are talking political will and what social philosopher Stuart Rees calls 'the creative use of power'.[108]

Imagine!

CHAPTER 3

Sustainability

One has to challenge people with the facts, for example, that in 2000 we spend 11 billion in Europe on ice cream a year which is about twice what it would cost to provide access to clean drinking water for people in poor countries.

(Chris Patten)[109]

Ecological awareness will arise only when we combine our rational knowledge with an intuition for the nonlinear nature of our environment.

(Fritjof Capra)[110]

Most current development fails because it meets human needs incompletely and often degrades or destroys its resource base.

(IUCN, UNEP, WWF)[111]

Sustainable development is an important entry point for corporate citizenship; indeed for many people it is the only place to begin when discussing the interface of business and society. In this case detergents, ice cream, water and the survival of the planet are intermeshed, if not synchronised. What is so surprising is that we have come to the planet so late, but perhaps we could not see it; perhaps we could not see the links between Omo, water, war and corporations.

When summing up the twentieth century the historian Eric Hobsbawm said:

The ecological problems, though in the long run decisive, were not so immediately explosive. . . . they tended to be to be mistakenly discussed in terms of imminent apocalypse. . . . But a rate of economic growth like that of the second half of the twentieth century, if maintained indefinitely, must have irreversible and catastrophic consequences for the natural environment of this planet, including the human race which is part of it.'[112]

So, like so many stories in the last 30 years we could start with the planet: with the sustainability of the natural environment. Clive Ponting's *A Green History of the World* has a chapter headed 'The rape of the world' in which he says: 'Over the last 10,000 years human activities have brought about major changes in the ecosystems of the world.'[113] For many activists and public policy makers, environmental sustainability is *the* starting point for any investigation of the relationship between business and society. It is argued that it is modern economics, guided and driven by large corporations, that has despoiled our planetary home. This fragile planet is degraded and degrading fast and we are at the point of no return. To save our souls we must first save the planet. Much of the action on corporate citizenship is therefore concerned with the use and misuse of environmental resources, with community rights to resources, with waste and environmental justice.

It is undeniable that we have a choice between either treading lightly on the Earth or pillaging and plundering environmental resources.

One of the profound benefits of using the state of the planet as an entry point for corporate citizenship is its modernist universality. Although most people do not understand the mechanics of global warming or our relationship to the destruction of the ozone layer, even the most desensitised urban person understands that clean water is better than polluted water, and that a good sanitation system is worth its weight in gold.

There is a universal belief in the prospect of clean water. A significant number of specific events in the twentieth century led to the development of intense scepticism about scientific modernism and the rationality of technological progress as being naturally good. These events ranged from the introduction of DDT, CFCs and asbestos, which were portrayed as inert, benign and somehow serving private needs and the common good, to the extreme use of industrialisation in developing intercontinental ballistic missiles, nuclear bombs and extermination gas chambers. In all these instances significant profits were made by private sector organisations, some of which are active today.

The other aspect of what postmodern philosopher Jean-Francois Lyotard has called 'the grand narrative' of modernist rational progress is that it has failed a significant minority of the world's population.[114] These 'others' have been left out of the story so far: 'Modernism assumed universality and left out the experiences and creations of women, non-whites and non-Western cultures'.[115] One way to understand the crisis that afflicts a third of the population of the world is to relate the statistics on poverty, degradation and destruction. Another way is through the telling of stories, through the everyday minor narratives that fix the attention of the listener or reader on the circumstances of the individual. Ironically this is also how we often come to understand the development of science (through knowing the person who made the discovery). This may account for the popularity of TV soap operas, because they often tell stories that we can all understand, in ways that we can all relate to. It may also account for the phenomenal increase in visitors to modern art galleries across the world. This may be countered by the idea that these temples to art have become 'somewhere to go' and Disneyesque in their experience. But it can be argued, their art helps the active viewer to understand a world that is not rational, scientific or obvious.

So it is that companies, realising the necessity to relate to us in both the grand narrative form and the lesser sub-text of life, tell us stories of liberation, empowerment and improvement alongside the statistics. Here is Unilever on the theory and practice of sustainability:

> A business like Unilever has a direct interest in sustainability. Unilever's long-term success depends on access to sustainable natural resources, particularly agricultural products, fish and fresh water. Water is the most fundamental necessity of life. Yet one third of the world's population does not have access to reliable, regular sources of drinking water – and the problem is getting worse. Water is also essential in our business. We need water to produce our products and the consumer needs clean water to use and consume them. No water: no washing, no cooking, no tea. It's as simple as that. [116]

Water

In *Surf's Up* the Beach Boys, a Californian rock band of the 1960s, advised us: 'Don't go near the water. . . . Our water's going bad.'[117]

The language of clean, accessible water is common everywhere: in Japan, Nigeria, Mexico, Germany, Scotland and in every place in the world. This may be why water is as good an example of the need to change our planetary management as any. In space exploration the possibility of there being water on planets and moons excites the imagination, as if such knowledge would mean there was also life there, as we know it on Earth. Surely, it is pointed out, whether our political system is capitalist or communist, autocratic or inclusive, it would be perfectly feasible and desirable to provide everyone with clean water!

Of the world's water, 97 per cent is in the oceans and the remainder is on land. Ice caps and glaciers contain 77 per cent of the land water, while 22 per cent is groundwater – most at more than 800 metres below ground level – and the remaining 1 per cent is in rivers and streams. But *we* are 75 per cent water. When we holiday many of us spend large sums of money to sit on a narrow strip of beach between the land and the ocean with few clothes on. Our relationship to water is full of love and fear. In *Apocalypse Now* the producer/director Francis Ford Coppola had an American military crew during the Vietnam War racing up river to find the reclusive Kurtz who had gone mad.[118] Joseph Conrad, on whose novel Coppola based his film, refers to the 'sleepless river' both in his metaphorical quest to the *heart of darkness* and in London where 'the traffic of the great city went on in the deepening night upon the sleepless river'.[119]

So many centres of urban life are based along rivers; so many corporate citadels look out over major rivers (including Unilever's on the Thames Embankment, almost opposite the Tate Modern). Now, like the rivers, the global economy never ceases flowing, 24 hours a day, 365 days a year. Water is in our blood.

And yet our inability to manage water resources globally kills 5 million people a year. It is worth reminding ourselves of how badly we manage this global issue: 40 per cent of the world's population (2.5 billion people) lack access to basic sanitation; 5 billion people will be without sanitation by 2025 through increased urbanisation; 5 million people die every year from diseases caused by unsafe water; 2 million die every year from water-related diarrhoea; 80 per cent of all disease in developing countries is caused by contaminated water, inadequate sanitation and poor hygiene; 50 per cent of all hospital beds in developing countries are occupied by patients suffering from waterborne diseases;

90 per cent of water is used for agriculture; and women, children and the poor are disproportionately affected by the lack of clean water. And yet most of these people live in countries with markets, some dominated by some of the same global corporate citizens who provide the stories for numerous texts on business and management.

Interestingly, some of the most significant writers on management and globalisation in the twentieth and twenty-first century fail to mention water. Peter Drucker does not mention it in his *Management Challenges for the 21st Century*, nor do Richard J. Barnett and John Cavanagh in *Global Dreams*, or George Soros in *The Crisis of Global Capitalism*. Even that chronicler of the twentieth century, Eric Hobsbawm, fails to mention water as an issue in the last century in *The Age of Extremes*.[120]

This is, of course, unfair. Or is it? Drucker's book says: 'This book is a call for action. . . . We live in a period of profound transition – and the changes are more radical perhaps than even those that ushered in the "Second Industrial Revolution" of the middle of the nineteenth Century, or the structural changes triggered by the Great Depression and the Second World War.' The book discusses the 'new social, demographic and economic realities' and argues that these cannot be dealt with by politics or free market theory, but only by 'management and the individual'. But nowhere does the book mention what is seen by some people as the single most important driver for change, namely our dysfunctional relationship to the planet we share and one of its prime constituents: water.

Barnett and Cavanagh's *Global Dreams* is heavy on shopping malls, corporations and international finance. It begins with the image of Spaceship Earth, which provides a 'unifying metaphor to awaken planetary consciousness', but does not then return to the image of home, survival, community and the sustainable environment.

Soros's critique of global capitalism is forceful and somewhat compelling, given that he has been one of the greatest financial beneficiaries of its manipulative processes. His concept of reflexivity calls for a change in the imbalance between an immature global political system that is no match for a rapacious global financial system that tends towards instability.

We know that the twentieth century was the century of industrialised warfare, in which millions of people on battlefields, in cities and in concentration camps were subjected to mechanised death. Many wars began through a desire for natural resources and territory. The Japanese invasion of China and push south in the 1930s was for oil, and the German invasions of their neighbours aimed to gain control of the territories of Europe. But also during this period millions of people died through the misuse of, or lack of access to, environmental resources, such as water, around the world.[121]

Water is used here to illustrate an obvious paradox. Water is only mentioned when money can be made from it: witness the sale of Wessex Water in the United Kingdom for some $1 billion to a Malaysian conglomerate, YTL, after the collapse of Enron in 2001, and the price of shares for the bottled-water company Evian in France. But as a global citizenship issue it should be paramount, and as a management issue surely it should be easy to solve? And don't all those companies that claim to be global corporate citizens, multi-local enterprises and caring community companies have a vested interest in the link between clean water and economic stability? The global non-bottled water business is estimated to generate annual revenues of US$300 billion for corporations.[122]

In 'The good and bad things in the world' (see box), my youngest daughter was expressing a *middle* way, where there is some integration between clean water, kindness, friendship and trees on the one hand, and being unkind to people, dirty water and polluting the atmosphere on the other. This could be described as sustainability, or, for Anthony Giddens, this is the *third* way: the renewal of social democracy. For him 'ecological modernisation' is one of the five dilemmas for social democracy: 'the notion of sustainable development fits well with the broader one of ecological modernisation'.[123] Ecological modernisation appears to mean upstream thinking: redesigning society on the principles of sustainability rather than unfettered growth; anticipation rather than cure and end-of-pipe solutions; pollution equalling inefficiency; and making a link between environmental regulation and economic growth – that is, of course, sustainable ecological growth.

Without conforming to Hobsbawm's ecological nightmare scenario related earlier, it is clear from the evidence that the ecological situation is grave. The United Nations Environmental Programme 2002 annual report states 'the environment is still at the periphery of socioeconomic development' and 'the level of awareness and action has not been commensurate with the state of the global environment today; it continues to deteriorate'.[124] The situation is confirmed by a WWF report: we have seen 'improvements in the quality of life for people in many parts of the world, yet we continue to exact an unacceptable price from the Earth's ecosystems at the same time'.[125]

Those who argue that the current neoliberal model of economic development has generally raised living standards are correct, but fail to recognise that there have been winners and losers, or that this model is ecologically unsustainable in the long run. There is also a failure to focus on the merits

---

The good and bad things in the world

My youngest daughter, when she was eight years old, was asked to write about the environment as part of a school project. She mentions clean water as one of 'the good things in the world':[126]

The good things in the world	*The bad things in the world*
trees	crisp packets
birds	sweet papers
animals	plastic bags etc
clean water	diseases
mud	getting killed
flowers	doing wrong
sun	polluting the atmosphere
sky	being unkind to people
wind	dirty water
rain	having no money
kindness	going to prison
fields	
grass	
friendship	

Cleo McIntosh
Newbridge Junior School, Bath, England
Summer 1994

Unilever's 0.1 per cent of global water use[127]

We estimate that our 'water imprint' – the total volume of water used to make and use our products – is equivalent to around 0.1 per cent of all the water extracted for use globally each year. Agriculture is the biggest user: we estimate that potentially half of our overall water imprint must be associated with growing the produce that accounts for three-quarters of our raw materials.

The world's water systems – a shared, finite but renewable resource – are under extreme pressure. More than 1 billion people lack access to safe drinking water. Unsafe water and poor sanitation cause an estimated 80 per cent of all diseases in the developing world. No single measure would do more to reduce disease and save lives in the developing world than bringing safe water and adequate sanitation to all.

Without major improvements in the way water is allocated, used (which means actions to reduce consumption and to minimise impact on water quality) – and *re-used* – the global water situation will get considerably worse over the next 30 years. Indeed, water will be the major impediment to development in the future in several regions.

At Unilever, our approach to water sustainability is based on understanding the water imprint of our operations locally and [on] ensuring that our imprint is sustainable within the limits of the relevant water catchments. For example, in the past five years we have cut water pollution loading from our factories by over 20 per cent. Many of our factories, particularly in developing countries, discharge no effluent at all due to investment in on-site waste treatment and water recycling facilities. We are working to help our suppliers and customers do the same.

At least four things are crucial: reflecting the full economic value of water in pricing; making water use more efficient by reducing pollution and increasing reuse and recycling; developing integrated and participatory frameworks for the management of water; and utilising knowledge and technology in partnership with local people. [We] believe the GATS negotiations in the Doha Round can and should do a lot to encourage more private investment and know-how in water treatment and recycling services.

unilever.com

of better environmental management in resolving conflict. For instance it has long been a truism of the Middle East situation that water is as crucial as oil in the politics of the area. According to recent estimates Jordan, Israel, the West Bank, Gaza, Egypt and the Arabian Peninsula all face water shortages. There is an obvious need to reduce conflict and manage the peace, and the development of stronger regional institutions could come about through focusing on water. After all water has the annoying habit of ignoring territorial boundaries: it is also vital to life and development.

General agreement concerning the state of the planet confounds postmodernists because the universality of planetary conditions is profoundly modernist in the sense that there may be some agreement concerning the *degraded* state of the planet. There may be universal agreement, although how we tackle it may present a diversity of strategies and attitudes. Ecology, as used here, could be called the *post* postmodernist modernism. The Tellus Institute, without referring to the largely intellectual dilemma of modernism and its critics, wrote of the twenty-first century being the 'planetary age'. After decades of the science of ecosystem understanding, after an array of astronauts staring back at Earth from space and wondering at the fragility and loneliness of planet Earth floating in the cosmos, and after the death of distance through electronic contact, now is the century where 'one world' becomes a political reality as well as a slogan for a global airline alliance: 'oneworld'™, which brings together airlines from the United Kingdom, United States, China, Ireland, Finland, Spain, Chile and Australia. As its publicity says: 'It's natural to want to be cared for. Because we work together as an alliance, the people from one member airline are always on hand to look after passengers from any other. Why? because oneworld™ revolves around you.'

One world, or an understanding of planetary ecology, is the end of modernism as we have known it. It is the evolution of a new modernism with shared ecologically based values, common principles for managing shared values, and sensitivity to and a celebration of the diversity of histories of the planet and people. Intercourse around ecology provides a platform for a liberating modernism that celebrates the 'other' within the confines of the physical carrying capacity of the Earth. This is what Ulrich Beck has called our 'ecological enlightenment'.[128]

In closing this section on sustainability as an entry point for corporate citizenship, let me quote from one of the more lucid texts on corporate

governance: the South African King Commission. It argues that the nineteenth century was concerned with entrepreneurialism, the twentieth with
management theory and the twenty-first is the century of governance,
particularly between people and people and between people and planet.
The world could learn from the African notion of Ubuntu: 'humanness'.
As the report says: 'The notion of sustainability and the characteristics of
good corporate citizenship can be found within the concept of sound
human relations in African societies'.

For former poet-President Leopold Sedar Senghor from Senegal, 'In
African society, technical activities are always linked with cultural and
religious activities, with art and magic, if not with the realm of the
mystical'.[129]

CHAPTER 4

Corporate Responsibility, Synchronicity and Complexity

The most important task today is to learn to think in a new way.

(Gregory Bateson)[130]

Where there are markets there will be winners and losers, prophets (prof-its) and losses. And where there are humans you will find flies and gods.

(Anon)

The world that companies face today appears to many observers to be considerably more complex, chaotic and dynamic than the world of previous eras. . . . Boundaries between companies have diminished as long supply chains, strategic alliances, joint ventures and partnerships of various types have evolved virtual and network organisations.

(Jorg Andriof and Sandra Waddock)[131]

Previous chapters have noted that there are varying approaches to corporate citizenship through the portals of governance, human rights, sustainability, accountability and economic history. The subject can also approached from the viewpoint of an investor, a consumer or any other stakeholder. Indeed the clatter of conversation around the role, scope and performance of corporations is nowadays incessant and ubiquitous. To many this has the characteristics of discourse: it is informed but diverse, intelligent but opinionated, positioned but open to discussion. It is also a characteristic of this debate that most partic-ipants hold a multiplicity of roles. Just as corporate social responsibility can be approached through brand, consumer, stakeholder or producer, so too participants have a tendency as they engage to move between their social roles as mothers, employees, investors, managers, consumers and victims.

It is worthwhile pausing to list the themes that now present themselves in the field of corporate citizenship:

1. The relationship between human activity and the natural environment, represented in the discourse around sustainable development.
2. Governance and accountability for – and transparency in – decision making in business and government.
3. The contrast between talking to people and talking to organisations, and the disconnect that occurs.
4. The relationship and discourse (and lack thereof) between the corporate business world, public policy making and local communities.
5. The development of networks, network organisations and universal values, and the clash with places and territory.
6. The use and abuse of power, and the apparent power vacuum in many contemporary global–local situations.
7. And, most confusingly, that sometimes things just seem to happen without due rhyme or reason. Either this means that nobody is willing or able to take responsibility or that the most powerful force is at play: synchronicity.

The complexity of corporate responsibility

The global situation calls for a new approach that recognises this synchronicity, the complexity of the subject and the diversity of starting points. For instance, two areas that have recently attracted significant attention and that represent the theory and practise of corporate social responsibility (CSR) are supply chain management and stakeholder governance.

In this exploration of complexity and CSR, I make reference to the discussion of complexity theory, which derives from the natural sciences. The seven points of interest in the list above point to three key issues in CSR: a non-mechanistic explanation of social responsibility phenomena, the unpredictability of outcomes and the multilayered complexity inherent in all social responsibility situations.

For many companies a first glance at their supply chains, or their place in supply chains, has led them to realise their situation for the first time and to be overwhelmed by the quality and quantity of amassed data. This kaleidoscopic view of their universes has increased an understanding of corporate risk, cost management, human rights responsibilities and compliance liabilities. On issues such as child labour, animal welfare and toxic chemicals, customers and other stakeholders have put pressure on companies to explain and account for the origins and production of goods. The case of BSE, or mad cow disease, in the United Kingdom has highlighted the need for traceability of meat products: an example of closer engagement by companies in supply chain management. The web of interactions and relationships has amazed many managers who had previously relied on a comfortable relationship with a trusted supplier, with few questions asked.

The same can be said of first engagement with a fuller range of stakeholders than investors, suppliers, employees and customers. Just as some companies have discovered that, for instance, they were unknowingly helping perpetuate child labour through sourcing, so too listening to a wider range of stakeholders has led to a re-evaluation of the relationship between the company and society. It has been a wake up call for managers and directors. The corporate world has come alive to the reality of stakeholder driven strategic management where value is seen to be created across a whole range of stakeholder partnerships, rather than simply for shareholders. As Jorg Andriof has said:

> The dynamic political, social, economic and environmental environment and the interconnectedness of each of its elements provides a compulsion towards what is known as stakeholder partnership building.[132]

Both supply chain management and stakeholder engagement produce two challenges to the linear view of the firm. Insights from both approaches blow apart traditional notions of control from a fixed point: they destroy the idea of command and control and in doing so they change traditional views of power. However, most of the texts on the new management instruments that require enquiry and action on stakeholder and supply chain engagement fail to mention that their full incorporation and adoption inevitably challenges the very basis of most companies and the competencies of modern managers.

Being attentive to the noises and sounds of society through the mechanisms of supply chain assessment and stakeholder consultation gives a feeling of impermanence and change. No longer can the centre hold as the corporation, its products and reputation are seen as in constant flux, swimming in a sea of connected incidents and processes. The physicist David Bohm has written of the flowing, unbroken wholeness of life and the biologist Alan Rayner has spoken of inclusionality – that rather than separate entities all matter is connected one with another to make one completeness.[133] It is the relationship between things, or points of seeming solidity, that corporate social responsibility is now addressing. Business is discovering autopoiesis: that corporations are living systems with positive and negative feedback loops, circularity and self-reference. They maintain their integrity and identity through a seeming autonomy as a living system; as part of an unbroken wholeness.

Within the discussion of CSR, the keys to reaching an understanding of this perspective are in the language of the discussion, the medium of transmission and the context of the debate. These components describe the ongoing discourse around the topic. Heisenberg observed that the observer affects and is part of the observation and the results. The level of complexity in any given situation lies in the eye of the beholder as an observer. The manager whose orientation is towards the minimalist philosophy that 'to measure is to manage and to manage is to measure' will often fail to feel nuance, ambience and context.

That management is now a complex task and that the global corporation is a complex entity is accepted as one of the common usages of the word 'complex'. 'Complex' refers to counterintuitive thought, which is perhaps difficult to understand and unpredictable. It can also refer to a non-masculine, non-rational approach to situations. Indeed the idea that life cannot be managed in a straightforward way smacks of feminine uncertainty and a lack of clarity. Complexity theory says that this is how the world is.

There may therefore be a link between dysfunctional social systems and business and government, as they are mostly run by men in black suits with educational backgrounds that discount the difficulties of predictability and stress the discipline of clarity and conformance.

Complexity theory

Complexity theory has arisen as an area of significant research and discourse in the natural sciences to explain the inexplicability of certain observed phenomena and to view a way of understanding single incidents as part and evidence of the whole. It has been popularised by such writers as mathematician Ian Stewart and his book *Does God Play Dice?* and corporate governance expert Robert Monks in *The Emperor's Nightingale*.[134]

In this book I am making reference to the complexity of most corporate social responsibility situations and in doing so drawing upon work carried out in the natural science on complexity theory, as it is now known.

Recently there has been a transfer of knowledge to social science. Cilliers (1998) has applied complexity theory to the social world, as has more recently Swilling (2002).[135] The Santa Fe Institute has continued its pioneering work in this field and in particular John Casti (2002) has applied the theory to business, as have Robert Monks (1998) and colleagues to the specific area of corporate governance. In redefining organisational behaviour Morgan (1997) and Hatch (1997) have also addressed complexity in organisations.[136] Reason and Goodwin (1999) have written of the relationship between complexity theory, action research practice and the emergence of complex wholes (integrated systems).[137] Blockley and others in engineering management have used complexity theory to improve the construction industry's assessment of risk:

> A systems approach, as an alternative to scientific reductionism, has been used to model complex systems. The scientific method is based on the idea that one can take a complex problem and break it down into component parts and tackle each part separately and quasi-independently. The obvious penalty of concentrating on the part of a problem is the loss of perspective on the whole, a lessening of awareness of relationship between parts of the problem.[138]

In this chapter we look at the possibility of using complexity theory to look at corporate social responsibility issues.

Surprise, surprise and Royal Dutch/Shell

One of the characteristics of the new complexity theory is that of surprise. For Royal Dutch/Shell this was expressed by the Chair, Cor

Herkstotter, in October 1996 after the disastrous global media treatment
of the company over the Brent Spar oil rig confusion and allegations of
the company's complicity in the Nigerian government's murder of
opponents to the government's and the company's policies in Ogoni in
1995. Herkstotter says that there was 'a ghost in the machine, that is
causing us (Shell) to make subtle, but in the end, far-reaching, mistakes'
in assessing developments'.[139] Put simply, as in many other cases before
and since, issues often arise for corporations that take them completely
by surprise. They are not on their radar screens: they are Exocet missiles
that arrive at top speed out of the mist and hit their targets even before
alarm bells have been sounded. The case of Shell in the 1990s (at the end
of the twentieth century) is often referred to, perhaps too often, but it
provides a useful paradoxical situation. Here was a corporation that was
famous for scenario planning, that had sponsored work such as *The
Living Company* by Arie de Geus, and had a reputation for the management of natural resources for humanity. In essence here was a company
that saw itself as a well-managed, humane organisation led by leaders
ostensibly interested in people, planet and profits.

De Geus wrote in the Epilogue to his book that 'over time, fewer and
fewer companies will live and work in an environment over which they
have much control'. He concluded that 'the company is a living being'
and that 'the decisions for action made this living being result from a
learning process'.[140] De Geus worked for Royal/Dutch Shell for 38 years
across three continents. As such he can be characterised as epitomising
the new global governors, the global elite.

An unintelligent organisation that refuses to learn, or is perhaps in
denial, normally has one control point. The intelligent organisation,
when seen as a complex adaptive system, by contrast recognises a diffusion of authority. This can lead to the perception of a loss of power and
authority by those people who would like to feel they are in control. This
may lead to them treating their colleagues and staff badly and seeking
radical changes to the organisation's structure, all which can as a conse-
quence bring about the destruction of the corporate culture through
lower morale, increased stress and poor motivation. Over the last few
decades management fads such as business process reengineering,
delayering and downsizing have often caused the demise of companies
and the ruination of good people's lives because those in control sought

to keep control by managing the organisation in isolation from the sea in which it swims.

In a failing organisation there is a tendency to break the organisation and its activities down into component parts in the hope of spotting the fixable problem. This is only useful when accompanied by the helicopter overview. It is similar to breaking water into its constituent parts – oxygen and hydrogen – neither of which bears any similarity to its original composition. This means that little value is gained by reductionism. A piece of wood can only be a chair if it is viewed as part of whole world of meaning and connectivity. In other words the sum of the parts is far greater than the parts themselves. The company that downsizes and delayers to save money will rarely succeed unless it also works smarter, for the work force will ineluctably become stressed and unproductive. This will lead inevitably to absenteeism and poor quality outputs.

A prime example of the beginnings of ruination of an organisation is when you hear that (a) staff have been told to pay for their coffee, (b) hospitality and/or the Christmas party have been cut, or (c) they have moved into smaller office space. Just at the moment when you want employees to think as an empowered community, to be creative and innovative – and to work a little harder – you hit them where it hurts most, in the significant comfort areas of day-to-day living. The petty decision of the managing accountant on one small issue such as coffee or office space may remove a brick and bring the whole edifice down. This could be seen as analogous to the often-quoted application of chaos theory that the flap of a butterfly wing in Beijing can stop the traffic in New York. It is the law of unintended consequences, or in many instances the tipping point.

The tendency to reduce an organisation to its component parts and attempt to solve problems with this perspective can only succeed if the company also looks outwards and learns more about its context. The question to ask is: how big is the lake in which we swim and what are its energies, diversities and connectivities? How diffuse is where I am now? How much of this organisation is in another organisation? (Try mixing multicoloured beans to find the answer to this question.)

Ben Zander, the leader of the Boston Symphony Orchestra, who was quoted in the introductory chapter, asks: 'What assumptions am I making that I don't know I am making?' The notion of surprise is at the

---

The ecology of humour

In the early days of computer technology there was a man who had a powerful machine, and he wanted to know whether computers could ever think. So he asked it: 'Will you ever be able to think like a human being?' The computer rattled and blinked, and finally printed out its answer: 'That reminds me of a story.'

(Told by Gregory Bateson, author of *Steps to an Ecology of the Mind* (1972), as retold by Fritjof Capra[141])

---

heart of complexity theory. Surprise can mean instability, but it can also mean paradox. Paradoxes arise from false assumptions, and are often the basis for some of the best jokes!

A situation occurred in a stakeholder consultation exercise involving a very significant company. The consultants were told to ask a range of community stakeholders how the company had measured up to the company's stated objectives: the mission, vision and values. The stakeholder consultation exercise began with a mapping exercise and the final list of consultees included local business people, local government, professional organisations, environmental groups, employees, schools and a sample of people in the street. The company in question was a significant employer in the region.

There were two overall reactions to the exercise, both of which were unexpected by the company that had managed the exercise at both a global and a local level. First, none of the consultees had seen the company's mission, vision and values statement before. While they were impressed when they did see it, their evaluation started at that point. Second, a similar exercise had been conducted the year before, but on the basis of open questions and without reference to the company's statement of vision and values. All the consultees complained that there had been almost zero feedback to them of the results of that exercise. It should be stated that overall most consultees thought that the company had performed relatively well against their stated mission, vision and values, so that is not the point of this story.

The first significant point is the assumption by the company that the community stakeholders would have seen, or indeed be interested in, the company's higher aspirations. Second is that the feedback, while in this instance positive about the company's performance, had not had a chance to feed back to the company. There were no receptive channels. This company prides itself on being 'intelligent'. But what is intelligence if you cannot hear? Until the consultants' report was delivered the company did not know that they were on a different page to the community for which they depended for their successful operations.

This company was lucky that when the feedback came it was positive and largely in favour of continued operations. But in many cases the inability to understand the connectivity of a company to location and community is disastrous. Surprise is easy today, indeed easier than ever before because of the use of technology and the democratisation of airspace and the ether.

9 11

If we take another complex situation where intelligence could have radically altered the outcome the point may become clearer. Apart from complex systems being apparently unstable, prone to paradox through false assumptions, there are two other characteristics of surprise in complexity theory. These are the difficulty of computing outcomes and evidence of emergent patterns. This is where complexity theory, which could be helpful in examining business in society, is at variance from chaos theory. Chaos theory suggests that incidents happen on a random basis and are unpredictable, hence the butterfly effect. Complexity theory acknowledges that situations may be unstable, and that small incidents can have significant consequences, but that in the maelstrom of connectivity, of swimming in the same sea, emergent patterns can be observed. These emergent patterns depend on relationships and relativities, and are still uncomputable and therefore a surprise but their emergent properties are insightful in themselves. Being insightful of emergence does not provide unavoidable truths in a modernist sense, but it can provide clues to future behaviour. In other words it keeps us on our toes, looking out for the unexpected.

Emergent patterns depend on connectivity and therefore context. The two management instruments mentioned earlier, supply chain management and stakeholder engagement, are attempts to contextualise decision making. They are deeply political activities, as they posit the company as a possible agent of change through engagement with situations previously seen as externalities and beyond the company's responsibility. So, the intelligent organisation is willing and able to modify the rules on the basis of new information that becomes available. This is not just the modification of behaviour on the basis of new information, but a constant re-assessment of the basis on which information is assessed. In a complex system no agent will necessarily have access to other information systems, so there is always the possibility of surprise and unpredictability.

This is exactly what terrorism has always thrived on, but in the past this has tended to be local. Now intelligent terrorists have learnt that they can disrupt global systems through simple discrete actions. For instance the US airline Pan Am was effectively brought to its knees by the explosion of Flight 103 in 1988 over Lockerbie, which killed 270 people. The adaptation of existing complex social systems was used to extraordinary effect by the terrorists who destroyed the World Trade Center in New York on 11 September 2001.

The men who flew those American Airlines planes into the twin towers bought their tickets on American Express. They trained at the best pilot schools, sent their e-mails via Microsoft's hotmail and drove their Fords to the airports. Osama bin Laden, while anxious to be seen as a poor incorruptible messiah, is from a wealthy Saudi family intimately engaged in the oil wealth of the world – and New York. If al-Qaeda were part of the 'Other' we would not have heard of them. They are the other side of the coin of modernity: we didn't look behind the mirror enough to see what was staring us in the face: that our practices have come back to haunt us.

The men who managed Enron were also part of the same global elite that flies, e-mails and drives, invests and follows a fundamentalist line as self-serving as Osama bin Laden's. Remember that President George Bush Snr said before the 1992 Rio Earth Summit: 'The American way of life is not up for negotiation.'

In the 24 hours up to 08.45 on 11 September 2002 more than $1.3 trillion was traded on foreign exchanges, with capital 'ricocheting across the globe

> Our technologies have become more powerful than our theories. . . .
> We can do with technology what we cannot do with science.
>
> (Paul Cilliers)[142]

instantaneously'. Post-1970s deregulation, liberalisation, the elimination of capital controls and the encouragement of cross-border financial transactions have led to a globalised economy that favours the fast, the alert and the avaricious at the expense of the traditional, the thoughtful and the slow.

In a sense the unpredictable was easier to deal with in a slower world and the impacts could be more easily contained. The globalisation of the economy and egalitarianisation of communications technology, coupled with the travel industry, have allowed access to complex systems heretofore controlled from centres of power. If you have malice 'it is anyone's world' as various computer viruses and al-Qaeda have shown. But it is also everyone's world in the way large corporations develop and sell new products. The Finnish telecom company Nokia has succeeded by exploiting the same developments as al-Qaeda.

The challenge then is to pinpoint emergent patterns that give an indication of developments one way or another. Recent research on complex systems has shown that there may be similarities between the spread of AIDS, Internet viruses and social development. In each case there are indications that growth is not random and that situations can be managed by spotting emergences. In all three cases it appears that knowing key points, or hubs or actors, can allow efforts to be better targeted even though the systems may be ongoing and uncontainable in their life patterns. For instance it appears that a computer virus can be destroyed by targeting key Internet hubs, that AIDS can be treated by locating the most promiscuous people, and that the unpredictability and variables of geography and world trade can be partially overcome through the development of robust social institutions.[143]

In the case of corporate social responsibility we may be nearer establishing what Malcolm Gladwell has called 'the tipping point'.[144] His thesis is that 'little things can make a big difference'. It was the anthropologist Margaret Mead who said that we should never doubt the impact that a small determined group of people could have on larger affairs.

In management and business theory the case of Honda's moves into the US market are often quoted as examples of the unpredictable driving innovation and change. Honda executives examining markets in California but lacking transport started driving arriving at appointments on 50 cc motor cycles and in doing so sowed the seed for the global development of the Honda motorcycle industry. They were the first Japanese auto manufacturer to set up a factory in North America.

One of the characteristics of complexity theory is that it has no universality beyond describing the characteristics of the theory. So, to paraphrase George Bernard Shaw, 'the golden rule is that there is no golden rule'.[145]

One contemporary philosopher of complexity theory is Paul Cilliers:

> There is no overarching theory of complexity that allows us to ignore the contingent aspects of complex systems. If something really is complex, it cannot be adequately described by means of a simple theory. Engaging with complexity entails engaging with specific complex systems.[146]

One of the problems for the corporate social responsibility movement relates to its efforts to develop instruments that will accurately account for and measure corporate behaviour and impact.

For instance the modelling of the world around corporate accountability systems such as SA8000 and the Global Reporting Initiative is a drift towards some sort of modernist universality that in its development and use finds it difficult to measure, let alone feel, context, unpredictability and conviviality. Roland Barthes wrote in the 1950s 'When will we write the history of men's tears?' This is why the global corporate citizenship movement is sometimes accused of a new imperialism. Surely, rather than trying to curb the power of large corporations we should curb the corporations themselves, so that their power is ours?

Cilliers, modelling Einstein's fears in the 1940s about our inability to handle the implications of atomic power, has said that: 'At the heart of the matter . . . our technologies have become more powerful than our theories. . . .We can do with technology what we cannot do with science.'[147] The same is true of our largest corporations. We can deal with soap but we cannot deal with Unilever. We can swim in a sea of new products but we cannot call our corporations to account for their delivery mechanisms.

The culture of humility

I have suggested that complexity theory might help us develop an intellectual framework for taking corporate social responsibility analysis forward and providing a practical methodology for managers. This framework will be based on what South African social philosopher and activist Mark Swilling has called a 'culture of humility'. In his case he is interested in finding greater cooperation between the sciences and the humanities, and he is specifically interested in using the complexity approach because of the humanistic issues of ethics in theory and practice. Swilling says:

> One key advantage of the complexity approach is that there is no basis for deterministic prediction. This is crucial for constructing a culture of humility because all claims to knowing anything must be qualified by the partial and provisional nature of what is known – in short, an appreciation and therefore admission of uncertainty. This, in turn, can help prevent the holders of power from using knowledge to create false certainties. If certainty cannot be derived entirely and exclusively from rational enquiry, this clears the way for more experiential reflection on the ethical basis for human action in specific contexts when intellectual knowledge is admittedly at best provisional and impartial.[148]

'The culture of humility' proposed by Swilling also helps with the accusation of ethical relativism as apparently practised by multi-national corporations around the world. They are sometimes accused of promoting mission, vision and values at the corporate global level but practising relativism on the ground in diverse community situations. So for instance they preach equal opportunities but are happy to divide their staff on different grounds when operating in Saudi Arabia. A corporation will reframe the ethical arguments about remaining in China, but disinvest from Burma, although both countries' governments have been accused of human rights abuses and undemocratic politics.

Humility does not mean that corporations that blatantly lie or are duplicitous can be let off the hook. There is still a need to call them to account, but there are many situations where the corporation is but one component in a supply chain, and the system needs looking at for its complexity and context. The corporation may not be the agent of repression, and its removal from a supply chain may not help remove the perceived oppression or abuse. Corporations being large and often unaccountable and impervious to criticism are easy targets, but again reducing a system to its component parts may reduce our ability to understand the nature of economic transactions, which are the agents of pro-human change, and may damage the weakest not the strongest participant in the process.

Much of this application of complexity thinking to corporate social responsibility is counterintuitive. For instance the author of *Fast Food Nation*, Eric Schossler, normally a strong opponent of the development of junk food around the world, particularly US junk food, has been heard arguing that the traceability of individual ingredients has been enhanced by McDonald's.[149] As a company they have globally insisted on being able to trace all their foodstuffs despite the fact that the US government has specifically resisted legislation in this area and European governments have been slow to act. For McDonald's this was a case of product liability, brand management and reputation assurance, not forgetting health and safety issues in the United Kingdom when it came to mad cow disease. In this case this company has advanced humanity through the diligent understanding of the complexities of bringing beef, bread and potatoes from field to mouth.

Before proceeding to look at how complexity theory might be useful in revisiting corporate social responsibility and drawing on what has been discussed so far it, is time to annotate the essence of the theory.

1. Complexity theory seeks to look beyond postmodernism, not by providing the universality of modernism but by providing an open approach to looking at any given situation.
2. In any given situation the whole is greater than the sum of the individual parts
3. The individual parts are never alone, but can only be recognised because of their relationship to other parts; in other words they can only be seen as parts of a whole.
4. In a complex system there are multiple interactions, connectivities, relativities and relationships, and this provides richly textured patterns.

5. The results are difficult to predict and are non-linear.
6. The specificities of context means that it is difficult to compute possible outcomes beyond establishing emergent patterns that might arise from direct and indirect feedback loops.
7. Complex systems are open to exchanges of information and energy, and can thus become intelligent.
8. Complex systems have learning and unlearning, change and uncertainty at their heart.
9. Because it is possible to detect emergent properties of complex systems it is possible to say that they have histories and memories. They become surviving adaptive systems through understanding their own histories.
10. The adaptive nature of complex systems means that they are unpredictable and uncomputable, but that it is possible to detect emergent but unspecified and unknown properties.
11. Complex adaptive systems may, therefore, evolve into new systems, merge with others or disaggregate.
12. One period of time may not allow an observer to recognise a complex adaptive system in another period of time, because it will have changed and taken on a new identity.
13. New forms emerge through networking and creative destruction, not through annihilation or survival of the fittest.
14. A distinction is to be made between simple, complicated and complex systems. Simple systems tend to be linear and 'dead', complicated systems are just that (complicated) and not open to adaptation or learning – unlike complex systems.

Paul Cilliers makes the point that a Jumbo jet is complicated, while mayonnaise could be seen as complex – by a French person! Another example, which exemplifies the idea that complexity, like beauty and love, is in the eye of the beholder, comes from John Fowles' novel *Daniel Martin*, where different nationalities are observing the pyramids in Egypt. For some they represent feats of technology and engineering, like Jumbo jets, others see works of art, and for others the pyramids have cosmological significance that goes far beyond the works themselves. In other words the pyramids are like the Hindu conundrum of the blind people encountering the elephant and having myriad experiences.[150]

So, there are three premises for this book, which link some aspects of complexity theory and the field of corporate social responsibility.

- First, corporations that survive have had to become complex adaptive systems. This is supported by the evidence in de Geus's *The Living Company* and Collins and Porras's *Built To Last*.[151]
- Second, that the link between the product and the corporation is an example of a complex adaptive system owned by no one, like a bee hive, and making new forms like an ant hill. On the one hand the driving process may be the market and the market institution – the incorporated company – and on the other hand, in the case of the supply, sale and consumption of a consumer good such as heroin, it is just the market.
- Third, corporate social responsibility is mostly concerned with identifying new complex adaptive systems by putting product, process and corporations into a picture of relationships, connectivities and convivialities. In other words the relationship between Unilever and Dove soap looks more like a Jackson Pollock painting than a Mark Rothko. At one end of a spectrum we have Warhol's soup cans; at another end Jackson Pollock; and at two other ends (there are no real endings or beginnings to complex adaptive systems), Hockney's parents and Picasso's *Guernica*. It is also multilayered like Beethoven's Fifth or Philip Glass's *Glassworks*.

So what can complexity theory teach business, and in particular how can it help us grapple with the 360 degrees of the corporate citizenship enquiry and issues of corporate social responsibility?

Stuart Kaufman at the Santa Fe Institute in the United States says that 'the fate of all complex adapting systems in the biosphere – from single cells to economies – is to evolve to a natural state between order and chaos, a gradual compromise between structure and surprise'.[152] It may be possible, he argues, to find a connection between evolution and business performance, using models of complex systems from the former and applying them to the latter. This notion of 'life at the edge of chaos' is also the theme of Danah Zohar's *Rewiring The Corporate Brain*.[153] Most organisational changes and social transformation programmes, she argues, simply shift the furniture around without changing the building.

The other side: the wandering mind

One of the world's most popular modern art galleries, the Tate Modern in London, is built in a disused coal-fired electricity power station on the banks of the River Thames opposite St Paul's Cathedral. Some of the exhibits, such as 'the pile of bricks' and Tracey Emin's unmade bed are controversial, to say the least. I told a colleague, who had spent a significant proportion of his life in the straight jacket of a multi-national corporate culture that I loved visiting the gallery. He was visibly shocked. I said I enjoyed it because it was like seeing the inside of my mind – there was some rubbish, some unexpected treats and some mediocrity – but it allowed my thoughts to wander off their normal tracks and I found this very refreshing and inspiring. In other words, the items on display got to parts of my brain that other mediums could not reach. He exclaimed that the inside of my mind must be in a bad state! I reminded him that Tolkien, author of *The Lord of the Rings*, had memorably said: 'Those who wander (or wonder) are not necessarily lost'.

The real paradigm shift that is necessary, to use Thomas Kuhn's phrase correctly, is to reject the notion there is a god-given form for anything, or that there are *a priori* conditions for building social systems and organisations. This theory does not support an 'anything goes' position either, just as it is not amoral and relativistic. What it is interested in is the proposition that patterns naturally emerge, based on relationships that are unexpected and unpredictable. In other words, natural order is constantly changing in the space between order and chaos. The points of change or transformation come at what Kaufman calls 'self-organised criticality'.

A good example is traffic gridlock in a city. There are innumerable variables, constant direct and indirect feedback loops, and human system interventions designed to direct the traffic (lights, roundabouts etc.), but on some days the whole system tips over into complete standstill. Gridlock. There are some patterns, but it is difficult to say where and when the gridlock will occur with any great accuracy. For town management, the problem – which operates in an apparently random fashion – is that there are so many disparate claims on space and the environment. Over coordination risks abuse in a democratic society, and totalitarian regimes do not seem to manage much better, perhaps because the complexity of the urban environment allows some degree of freedom in an oppressive society.

We are extrapolating complexity from science to social systems. Some scientists have recognised that science needs to be holistic to understand itself. In the past it has traditionally attempted to fix knowledge through the use of experimental evidence to verify theories, allowing multiple sceptics to repeat experiments within rigidly controlled boundaries. This leads to the reinforcement of scientific theory. However, large portions of human experience, and dare we say knowledge, are discounted because they cannot be replicated and tested under the same conditions. This means that there is a tendency to dismiss some enquiry as unscientific and irrational. What management theory has discovered is that managing people (human capital being the most important component in the post-industrial economy) requires taking the irrational seriously, and making context the key to understanding motivation.

Postmodernism is derided by some as undisciplined and constantly revisionist but, as philosophers such as Zygmunt Bauman have argued, postmodernism actually requires greater rigour on the part of those who reach ethical positions, precisely because it requires rigorous analysis of different positions.[154] Similarly, while Lyotard argued that modernism and consensus lead to a lack of richness and deny the texture of human experience, there is a meeting point in postmodern theory and complexity theory where both recognise the shifting sands of analysis and discourse through constantly reassessing the incoming information provided through ongoing feedback.[155] In other words postmodernism and complexity reach the same conclusion, that *patterns* of behaviour, belief and values emerge in complex adaptive systems.

So the complex adaptive system that is the supply chain from field to mouth in which McDonald's plays an important part (in some parts of the world) is open to learning, unlearning, networks and action. Action can be brought about by customers deserting to Burger King, by protestors causing the company to improve their recycling policies, and by governments demanding health warnings on all burger sales. And this constant updating and adaptation may lead to dialogue but not necessarily consensus.

Corporate *social* responsibility, ethics and society

Returning to the original propositions at the start of this chapter, I want to argue that most of the corporate social responsibility debates are just that: social, rather than specifically business. Most of them conform to the characteristics of complexity theory, and, as contained discourses, they are often embedded in complex adaptive systems. The level of interaction is normally rich and heavily textured, non-linear and unpredictable, and there are many interconnections. And the individual elements are ignorant of the behaviour of the whole system, but dependent on each other for their dynamism.

Society can be seen as a complex, self-organising system with the characteristics of evolution rather than transformation, because of the nature of unpredictability and uncomputability created by random feedback loops. We are not disinterested observers, but rather active participants for whom, as part of humanity, there are supreme ethical considerations. Nature may feed back decay or mutation, and we are part of that feedback, but we also feed back social concerns, some of which are transcendent: that is part of what it means to be human.

Therefore, returning to the issue of ethical judgement and the universality of moral positions, which many large corporations have adopted – how should they now act? If relativism is laziness, if corporations are themselves complex adaptive systems and part of larger systems, and if we cannot discount the concept of transcendent ideals to which we can aspire (even though they have universality, which can be seen as antithetical to the idea of a learning system) how should we act?

I quoted previously Shaw's aphorism that the golden rule is that there are no golden rules; most of the world's religions accede to the demand that you should love your neighbour *as yourself*, that universal rules should not make for intolerance. Perhaps, therefore, an advance on the nihilism of relativism, and of the perceived irresponsibility of postmodernism can be replaced with an action and enquiry position derived from complexity theory. Some starting points would be those given below.

The culture of humility code

- Recognise that as a participant you and your beliefs are fallible: show humility.
- Responsibility means being an active participant in judgements, and therefore requires effort and the recognition that universality can be equated with laziness.
- Respecting diversity, otherness and difference is a value in itself.
- Gather as much information as possible, while recognising that it will not be possible to gather all the information.
- Consider the consequences of the judgement, while recognising that it will not be possible to consider all judgements.
- Do not dig too deep a hole; make it possible to reverse the judgement if needs be, if the information changes or if the theory is found to be flawed.[156]

This approach supports one of the fundamental tenets of corporate citizenship: that corporations should be able to articulate their role, scope and purpose on an ongoing basis.[157] It also supports the structuration theory of sociologist Anthony Giddens because it combines macro and micro theory with his definition of post-modernity (rather than post-modernism). Giddens' modern modernity says that we live in reflexive times where we continually question how we got here and what its all about, but it is not post-modern. This questioning provides conversational feedback loops, à la Luhmann and Habermas, that make up modern modernity and differentiate us from traditional societies where autopoeitic reflection is not the norm.

We live in interesting times, but an era in which the search for meaning is ever more crucial for many people. Satish Kumar, the Director of Schumacher College in South Devon in England, tells the story of the numerous people who attend programmes at the college. Many have reached a reflective stage in their lives, perhaps in their forties and upwards, and they are asking questions about the purpose of life, often having been on the treadmill of organisational work. Schumacher College does not run psychotherapy sessions but it does run a series of programmes on connectivity, sustainability, art and spirituality with clear links to the work of E.F. Schumacher.[158] There is then little need for psychotherapy.

'You must be the change that you wish to see' (Gandhi)

People, planet and prosperity: olives, oranges and humanity

There is a hotel on the Greek Peloponnese, just an hour's fast boat trip across the Adriatic from the steaming, dusty city of Athens. It is run by two brothers who have simplicity and lifestyle as their mission and vision. The small hotel is on the waterfront, and looks out across the Adriatic towards misty islands. The bedrooms are simple; there are no televisions and the telephones were disconnected many years ago. The restaurant serves the simplest of food made from the most local and basic ingredients: the dishes all taste of the herbs that grow on the nearby hills. The brothers are interested in customers returning and maintaining the ambience of the hotel. They close for five months of the year, and in October collect organically grown olives from their local olive grove to make the best of oil, which they use in the hotel, and sell to the local growers cooperative. They also have a small organic orange grove. When visitors to the hotel leave the hotel they are given olives and oranges to take home as a gift from the brothers.

After the most wonderful relaxing stay looking out over the azure blue of the Adriatic and visiting the world's largest outdoor amphitheatre – 2,500 years old – to be given a present of such authenticity and humanity by your hosts creates the most exquisite feeling and continues the holiday back home until the olives and the oranges are finished. A year later we are still travelling back to that hotel as we slowly eat the olives one by one. In this case one plus one equals peace and happiness.

The point of the story concerns the brothers. They have travelled, and in fact grew up in Toronto, Canada. Their participation in a local archaeological dig uncovered a small village amphitheatre, a mirror of the theatre at Epidaurus. This led them to think about their hotel, their guests, olives and oranges, and to make connections about how they could help bring peace and harmony. The manner in which they run their hotel is their answer. There is no spiritual overload or dogmatism and visitors should not expect miracles - the change comes from being

> away from the hurly burly and in touch with ourselves. The brothers are just carrying out Mahatma Gandhi's maxim in their business: 'You must be the change that you wish to see'.
>
> Tour companies come and go and try to subvert them, take-over offers are ignored and guest keep coming back! This is (a) good business.

I have said that one of the major problems at the heart of the corporate social responsibility industry is that often too much emphasis is put on the business element. Sure, there is a need to confront the excesses of the market and capitalism does breed greed and dysfunctionality, but CSR can only be tackled by adopting a social perspective and seeing the context in which business operates.

Cities, organisations, communities and the UN Global Compact

This can be exemplified by the UN Global Compact principles – originally built on the idea of making business humane by bringing together business and the UN's moral mission – which have been adopted by the Australian city of Melbourne.[159] The City has used the nine principles, which cover human rights, labour issues and the environment (see list in box below), to convene community-wide meetings of multiple stakeholders to establish a common values platform for the management of the city.

Other examples of modelling complex communities include work carried out by Richard Rogers' partnership on sustainable cities. Many cities exist on the edge of chaos. For instance his team was able to use computer modelling in their designs for a major development in Shanghai, China. Making use of 'the complex matrix of criteria that make up the modern city', Rogers' team was able to measure 'the impact strategies on energy consumption, transport needs, parking requirements, pedestrian movements and the optimisation of sunlight'.[160]

Gareth Morgan applied the metaphor of flux and transformation to organisational form, which can mean a city or a corporation, to better

---

The next 100 years

The city of Melbourne celebrated its support for the UN Global Compact at a gala dinner on 9 October 2001 attended by over 850 senior business executives and members of the academic and diplomatic communities. The event, sponsored by the Committee for Melbourne, was billed as a glimpse into 'Windows of the Future: The Next 100 Years'. Keynote speaker and Committee for Melbourne Chairman Jack Smorgon, one of Australia's most accomplished business leaders, cited the Global Compact as an ethical touchstone for the evolution and growth of Australia's economy.

'Many of you would not be aware that Melbourne has become the first city in the world to engage the United Nations-sponsored Global Compact,' Smorgon explained. 'We have practiced what UN Secretary-General Kofi Annan has preached, by signing up to the nine values the United Nations has set out for companies globally to enhance their role in contributing to the quality of their community.'

---

understand 'emergent properties triggered by marginal adjustments' if observation is made of nonlinearity and randomness.[161] With this perspective, 'the manager acting with insights on chaos and complexity theory cannot be in control of the change'.[162] He invites managers to think about how the theories of autopoiesis, chaos and complexity show that change is an unfolding process of feedback, or patterns of interaction.

Most new corporate citizenship initiatives could be seen as based on this same principle: that an understanding can be reached concerning the relationship between business and society through observing emerging patterns of behaviour, but never any clear sense of certainty. Most of the new mechanisms for managing social responsibility, however, are sold to corporations and managers as giving greater control and more certainty by reducing risk and measuring the manageable, and vice versa. This is of course the Taylorist mode of organisational understanding with its linearity and command and control. But it may be antithetical to an 'edge of chaos' approach to management.

**The nine principles of the
UN Global Compact**[163]

The strategic goal of the Global Compact is to encourage the alignment of corporate policies and practices with internationally accepted values and objectives. The core values of the Global Compact have been distilled into nine principles in the areas of human rights, labour standards and the environment. These principles are drawn from three internationally recognised declarations.

Business should:

In terms of human rights:

1. Support and respect the protection of internationally proclaimed human rights within their sphere of influence.
2. Make sure that they are not complicit in human rights abuses.

In labour relations:

3. Uphold the freedom of association and the effective recognition of the right to collective bargaining.
4. Help bring about the elimination of all forms of forced and compulsory labour.
5. Help bring about the effective abolition of child labour.
6. Help eliminate discrimination in respect of employment and occupation.

In the environment:

7. Support a precautionary approach to environmental challenges.
8. Undertake initiatives to promote greater environmental responsibility.
9. Encourage the development and diffusion of environmentally friendly technologies.

So how can this approach help unpack corporate social responsibility? Just as Rogers and Partnership have been modelling communities around the world using complex modelling exercises with random feedback loops, so too complexity theorists have been modelling other social systems. One example among these is work at the Santa Fe Institute in California on possible changes in the occupancy of a bar depending on the expectations, feedback and limited knowledge of 100 people, and the modelling of an artificial stock market. These pieces of research led to the emergence of patterns and an understanding of both emergence and patterns that has been termed 'an ecology of predictors'.[164]

A further example of a limited complex adaptive system is a General Motors factory in Fort Wayne where a manufacturing model uses complexity to increase efficiency and reduce waste and use of resources. In the plant a finished truck approaches ten possible paint modules. Each module is geared to bid for the truck paint job, and the whole system has been geared to make each module paint as many trucks as possible and use as little paint as possible without regard for the other nine modules. In other words this is an example of local knowledge and applied intelligence. The plant receives bids from as many modules as have space and makes a decision as to speed and resource use. As each system is intelligent it learns to update its memory and revise future bids, which leads to the fastest possible work rate and the lowest possible paint use. GM reckon that this system saves $1.5 million a year over their previous linear system. The unpredictability of the approach has meant that so far it has been impossible to predict which paint module will win bids.[165]

A significant contribution of the application of complexity theory to corporate governance and corporate social responsibility has been made by Robert Monks in *The Emperor's Nightingale*. In this book he says that 'the modern corporation is poised for change through increased activism from shareholders'. In Europe and the rest of the world, one might speak of 'increased activism from a range of stakeholders, including shareholders'. According to Monks, 'humankind and all its creations struggle to reconcile the predictable and the dynamic . . . and this is the nature of the corporation, a human creation of special importance . . . an artificial life form'. The corporation is a complex adaptive system with both regularities and dynamics. The regularities are 'the drive for unlimited life, size, power, and license. The dynamics are 'multiplicity, spontaneity, accommodation, adaptation, transcendence, and metamorphosis'. This means, says Monks, that 'an aggressive management that is compelled by its shareholders to function within government-determined limits on externalisation will generate superior (financial) value over the long term'.[166]

Under the current model, 'the nuances of social responsibility (to a wider range of stakeholders than just shareholders) are considered to be appropriately reflected in the value accorded to corporations in the market'.[167] Whereas corporations had up until now represented themselves as machinelike systems 'bent on non-human principles – profit seeking missiles', Monks now sees hope in the application of complexity theory to the behaviour and analysis of corporations. If they are seen as having all the characteristics of complex adaptive systems, as described in this chapter, then they may be capable of metamorphosing into humane bodies if they receive the necessary feedback from society. This is not a moral position, he argues, but an inevitability given the current state of chaos on corporate governance. What he hopes to find in the application of complexity theory to business is 'the restored corporation': unpredictable, uncomputable, dynamic *and* humane.

But we have to see corporations as a human product, we have to stop viewing them as machinelike, and we have to make a balance between order and chaos, or regulation and dynamism, and most important between natural ecology and humane systems.

What organisations can we design that observe the fundamental boundaries of our planetary existence, recognise the limits, aspirations and materiality of humanity, *and* are creative, dynamic and adaptive? This is the challenge for the twenty-first century.

CHAPTER 5

The Complex Business of Corporate Responsibility

It is time to bring the rules that protect people and the planet to the core of decision making.

(Dr Vandana Shiva, Director, Research Foundation for Science, Technology and Ecology, New Delhi, India)[168]

It is a matter of understanding where the power actually lies. The reality is that however business is done in the world, it is inter-connected.

(Sir John Browne, CEO, BP, non-executive director SmithKline Beecham and Intel 2000)[169]

The basic program of the corporations as self-seeking entities wars against the interests of human beings. Yet the living 'complexity' of corporations – their tendency towards multiplicity, spontaneity, accommodation, adaptability, transformation, and metamorphosis – links corporations to us humans . . . for we too are complex adaptive systems.

(Robert A. G. Monks)[170]

Evolution is chaos with feedback, which gives us complex patterns. Our organisations and our systems of orderliness are like snowflakes. Snowflakes, beautiful to the human eye, are in a state of nonequilibrium and bound by the energy of metamorphosis between one state and another. Each is unique but they display patterns, patterns that are replicable in science but not computable in nature, each flake being different.

Modern organisations and capitalism assume more order than there is. They assume the free flow of information, the making of rational choices and that orderliness can prevail if there is control. They assume power can reside in one place, and that it can hold. They assume too that the natural ecological home of social organisations, planet Earth, is so benign and motherlike that it will succour dysfunctional organisational misbehaviour ad nauseam.

This chapter is concerned with the sustainability of human existence on planet Earth. It suggests that there are two approaches that should be utilised in conjunction in order to bring about a more harmonious co-existence of people and people, and of people and planet. The nexus between people and planet is prosperity, how we define it, how we make it and how we use it. The strapline for the 2002 Johannesburg World Summit on Sustainable Development was just that: 'People, Planet and Prosperity'.

The two approaches are a human virtue and an analytical tool. The first is humility towards our planet and towards each other: we do not know everything and we must not judge each other too harshly. The second involves humility in understanding how we live on this planet through the use of the developing eye of complexity theory.

Why advocate this tool? There are a number of aspects to complexity theory that may help us understand our relationship to the planet *and* understand our relationship with one another *within the same analytical framework*. Key to this approach is taking models that have already been developed in applied natural science and applied social science. For instance complexities of organisational change have been studied, as have the workings of the international finance system and the spread of BSE (mad cow disease). These analyses coupled with an understanding of the patterns that are emerging from the Internet and the life cycle of cities, for instance, can help us to build truly integrated models for planning a sustainable future.

I have already cited the modelling for sustainable cities, and this technique can be applied to other human systems involving business, government and civil society *and* planetary reconciliation.

The features of complexity theory that are attractive in attempting to develop a holistic methodology for looking at corporate social responsibility issues are holism, connectivity, intelligence, learning, context and renewal. Most important, business, like government and civil society, is but one component in a universe over which managers may think they have control. They may have some, but the power is constituted in a different form; it is neither Darwinian nor deterministic.

In short:

- The whole is greater than the sum of the individual parts.
- The individual parts can only be recognised because of their relationship to other parts.
- In a complex system there are multiple interactions, connectivities, relativities and relationships, and this provides richly textured patterns.
- The results cannot be predicted and are non-linear.
- The specificity of context means that it is impossible to compute possible outcomes beyond establishing emergent patterns from direct and indirect feedback loops.
- Complex systems are open to exchanges of information and energy, making them intelligent.
- Complex systems become surviving adaptive systems through understanding their own histories.
- New forms emerge through networking and creative destruction, not through annihilation or survival of the fittest.

This approach to problems is not impossible, but it does require re-seeing the world – learning, unlearning, networks and action. As Vandana Shiva and John Browne, quoted at the top of the chapter, say from different perspectives – physics and civil society activism in Shiva's case and geology and business in Browne's – connectivity is the key to understanding and humility.

It is interesting to note how the debate has developed and grown since the publication of Barbara Ward's book *Progress for a Small Planet* in 1979:

> The hope of a post-imperialist society in which sharing, common policies, and mutual support come to influence the habitual relations of government is not wholly in vain. If the powerful had never been ready to compromise, modern industrial society would never have achieved even a modest measure of social democracy and civil peace.[171]

We still have some way to go in developing a post-imperialist world, and there are many areas of the world where the legacy of oppression is still a current reality: I think particularly of places like South Africa, Ireland and Australia.

Wangari Maathai, a biologist and winner of numerous international awards for her work involving women in Kenya, seeks to use lessons of science and technology for the good, rather than the enslavement of people. She talks of a pyramid of wealth and oppression with the people from the poor South tending to be at the bottom of the pyramid.

> Upon birth, we began a journey which should lead to happiness and fulfilment. That is the purpose of all our efforts. Between birth and death, however, there are many obstacles which separate us from that goal. Some are natural, but most are made by humans. . . . Science and technology can sometimes lighten the burden, but do not seem to be doing so. Perhaps part of the problem lies with people themselves. Humans have to reassess their understanding of the universe and perception of what constitutes happiness. We may have to reassess systems of governance and seek security and peace not in a pyramid but in a balanced and harmonious whole.[172]

The constituents of an approach that marries natural and social science through the science of complexity requires a common language, and sometimes some silent reverence too as the immensity of the problem is understood. For those who have learnt to rely on predictability, certainty and replicability the challenge of replicability *plus* context produces patterns, and not absolution through answers and certainty. It sounds unlike science as it has been known. For those who are scientifically illiterate (which includes many of us) – but who know that life is about uncertainty, choices, intuition and surprise – conversations with those who hold rationality above uncertainty are difficult. The rationalists are frustrated by what they see as the lack of clarity of the other group, while the humanists are frustrated by being blinded by a science that often fails to contextualise or humanise. It is also often the case that natural scientists can converse with social scientists, but that social scientists are quickly confused by science. C. P. Snow was right In 1959, and today we still largely have 'Two Cultures'.[173] But there are significant moves to accept that this is a dangerous way to make public policy.

Sustainability, complexity and corporate responsibility

Chapter 3, on sustainability, assessed the evidence that by the early years of the twenty-first century there had been some significant gains in some parts of the world in environmental wealth and health, and in most parts of the world in democratisation. But we are still living beyond our means in terms of environmental wealth *and* some 25 per cent of the world's population are barely surviving. We are spending both the interest and the capital, to use the language of economics, and a significant proportion of the world's population are not able to establish decent, fulfilled lives.

There are some guides to the future that utilise many of the characteristics of complexity theory and are grounded in application and thorough research. The intention in applying this methodology to corporate social responsibility is to integrate perspectives representing people, planet and prosperity.

Examples of this system can be found in Morgan, who uses it to analyse the 'mad cow' phenomenon in the United Kingdom (which began in the late 1980s and still has consequences many years later) as a rich picture composed of 'loops rather than lines'. [174] The collapse of confidence in British beef, despite government assurances of its safety, led to the destruction of nearly 5 million cattle – almost all of which were free of the disease. Morgan cites similar extreme examples: the fall of US President Nixon over the Watergate burglaries in 1974, the Challenger space shuttle disaster, the disintegration of the Soviet Empire after the fall of the Berlin Wall in 1989.

In the same way, seemingly insignificant events can feed back into personal situations and have significant effects: one night of indiscretion leads to the break-up of a family and the end of a long marriage. The same understanding of feedback loops can be applied to situations that presented themselves to Royal Dutch/Shell in 1995 over the Brent Spar oilrig and in Nigeria over the murder of Ogoni activists by the Nigerian government also in 1995.

The Worldwatch Institute publishes an annual compilation of discrete analyses of 'environmental trends that are shaping our future'. The 2000/2001 edition made a link between the rises in several diseases. Specifically they said that the development of AIDS was linked to an increase in TB, which in turn was linked to an upswing in global tourism and a dramatic increase in refugees around the world, as well an increase in prison populations where disease often breeds.[175] This rich picture includes disease, geography, sexual activity, tourism, prisons and refugees.

In *A Systemic Approach to Sustainability Analysis*, Bell and Morse use the UK city of Norwich to develop a soft systems approach that can enable the 'drawing out of what might be major tasks and issues'.[176] This model-ling takes in: eco-decline in the region, new city industry and population growth, sustainability as public local policy, the historic city and the need for continuity, participation in consultation processes by the community,

---

The sustainable city

In planning for sustainable cities the process is as complex as it gets. Richard Rogers, advisor to the British government and award-winning architect, says that the Sustainable City is:

- A Just City, where justice, food, shelter, education, health and hope are fairly distributed.
- A Beautiful City, where art, architecture and landscape spark the imagination and move the sprit.
- A Creative City, where open-mindedness and experimentation mobilise the full potential of its human resources and allow a fast response to change.
- An Ecological City, which minimises its ecological impact, where landscape and built form are balanced and where buildings and infrastructures are safe and resource-efficient.
- A City of Easy Contact, where the public realm encourages community and mobility and where information is exchanged both face-to-face and electronically.
- A Compact and Polycentric City, which protects the countryside, focuses and integrates communities within neighbourhoods and maximises proximity.
- A Diverse City, where a broad range of overlapping activities create animation, inspiration and foster a vital public life.[177]

the development of sustainability indicators, global influences, global warming, and tourism.[178]

The practical realities of Rogers model (outlined in the box) for sustainable cities are easy to spot. This aspirational model has everything: a small ecological footprint, accessibility, community, happiness, conviviality, art and justice. The clashes between science, represented by technical possibilities, and community desires require both an understanding of technical limitations and a language of learning and discussion. This model contains different views of prosperity. A prosperous city is a diverse city? So let there be mobility, in and out, from across the planet? A prosperous city has equal rights to education and health? So ban all private medicine and education facilities? A prosperous city is an accessible city? So ban private vehicles?

The modelling for cities built on these lines is based on principles of equality and fairness, and the potential for lives to be lived in 'happiness and fulfilment'. The arrangements for developing such cities (and there are some that are half way towards this model) are the rigorous application of open access to consultation processes, a lack of corruption, technical and sustainability literacy, and an expectation of continual iteration and answers that are both unpredictable and unrestricted by any particular creed, whether scientific, technical, social or religious.

The challenge in modelling the complexity of CSR issues is to incorporate people, planet and prosperity in rich pictures. The Worldwatch Institute has over the years catalogued differences in resource use between varying countries, and it is clear that it is not the technology that is lacking in moving towards the dematerialization of society, but the political will.[179] Even a shift towards a knowledge economy, which many thought would lead to significant dematerialization, has led to an increased environmental footprint for the world's largest economy, the United States.

Many of our largest economic institutions are privately owned and geared to rewarding shareholders, even if we are stakeholders in this ownership process by virtue of our pensions, life savings and insurance policies. This means that under the current system the shift from sustainable business to sustainability is going to mean more than a semantic debate over the use of the word 'sustainable'. The scepticism over terminology is well articulated by the World Business Council for Sustainable

Development's *Walking the Talk*.[180] The WBCSD approach does accord with the view that the discourse around sustainability is concerned with social justice, the equitable distribution of and access to environmental resources, and futurity: the effect of decisions made now on future generations. 'Sustainable development cannot be achieved in only one sphere, such as the economic sphere. It will require types of partnerships never before witnessed in human history.'

Factor Four listed hundreds of products and processes that could be utilised now, using current technology, to reduce environmental resource use by a factor of two and increase wealth by a factor of two.[181] The theory and the practice were endorsed by commentators worldwide, from the British Prime Minister's Office to *Nature*, the *Economist*, and the *Financial Times*, so why is progress so slow? The answers lie in two interrelated areas. First, power lies with those who benefit most from the current system. As Walter Stahel at the Product-Life Institute in Geneva has said: 'Manufacturing industry is responsible for the manufacturing quality of its products, not its usefulness or disposal. Sustainable production implies a "cradle to grave" approach to legislators and economic actors, instead of a disposal optimisation of wastes.'[182] While financial profitability relies on the externalisation of environmental degradation from the business cycle and we are all dependent on it, what incentive is there to change?

Former Vice President Al Gore said of the US people, 'we are like addicts forever raiding the fridge when it comes to environmental resources'.[183] It is habitual. Stahel and colleagues have five pillars to their understanding of sustainability: nature conservation, health and safety (toxicity), reduced flows of matter (quantitative), social ecology (social structures and capital), and cultural ecology (education, knowledge, ethics and culture).

I have referred earlier to Robert Monks' prognosis that the current form of the corporation is doomed – or we are. As he says:

> The basic program of the corporations as self-seeking entities wars against the interests of human beings. Yet the living 'complexity' of corporations – their tendency towards multiplicity, spontaneity, accommodation, adaptability, transformation, and metamorphosis – links corporations to us humans . . . for we too are complex adaptive systems.[184]

Peter Senge, guru of organisational change at MIT, is also confused by our seeming inability to grapple with the changes that are necessary in our frozen corporate structures. 'One of the great mysteries of our current state of consciousness is how we can live in a world where absolutely nothing is fixed, and yet perceive a "fixedness".'[185] If we can see ourselves as part of the unfolding universe, this changes management in organisations profoundly. He advocates a commitment to being rather than doing, the latter coming from a commitment to the former.

> I actualise my commitment by listening, out of which my 'doing' arises. Sometimes my greatest acts of commitment involve doing nothing but sitting and waiting until I just know what to do next. . . . In most organisations today, managers who adopt this attitude would be considered non-managers because they are not doing anything to fix problems.[186]

The Santa Fe Institute has used the concept of complex adaptive systems to map stock markets, road-traffic networks, evolutionary systems, supermarkets, national economies, health-care delivery networks and the insurance industry.[187]

This chapter began by citing two examples of dominant management technology currently advocated by the corporate social responsibility movement: supply chain assessment and stakeholder engagement. They both give the manager a new view of the complexities of management. The manager may then do as Peter Senge advocates: sit and wait until they know what to do next. This may, of course, be because they are overwhelmed by the quantity of information. But this will only be a problem where there is a lack of integrity in the organisation. By integrity I mean meaning, vision, value and mission in the organisation. Vision and value give focus to work (and to daily lives). Where they are present the manager knows what to do with the new information gleaned from an exhaustive supply chain audit and an engrossing stakeholder consultation process. This is only true in a few organisations.

The organisation that is run from a central control on a bureaucratic basis with little internal creativity, engagement or mindfulness will be confused by the newly amassed information. Indeed it may cause the organisation to implode if it actually comes to understand what the external environment is saying to it.

Slime mould

A colleague told me a story from the natural environment. Alan Feest is a
leading expert on slime moulds, akin to fungi. He can often be heard on
BBC radio talking enthusiastically about their sex and reproductive lives.
But this is specialisation with a difference.[188]

He says that modern organisations should be thought of as slime
moulds. (Can you visualise your place of work as a heap of food-seeking
moving slime?) The ancient Greeks thought that the fast growth of
mushrooms was a sign of the natural spontaneity of life: that life can
come from nothing. After the rain it is not uncommon to see mushrooms
and other fungus appear as from nowhere, growing as you watch with
incredulous breath. Slime mould is similar to fungus in the way it grows
and metamorphises.

In slime mould, as in fungus, there is no centre and no cells. The edge
of the organism is in charge. This could lead to very serious jokes about
the 'edge of chaos' and 'the chaos of edges', but to continue . . . The fact
that there is no centre means that membranes on the external surfaces of
each slime mould sense the external environment – for food, danger, copu-
lants – and send signals to each and every nucleus in each cell. They are
literally inside-out organisms. Their eating patterns follow a similar
pattern. They excrete enzymes that pre-digest their food externally before
they absorb the nutrients internally. The key to their being is to be found
in the maintenance of the integrity of information flows within the organism. The whole organisation must have access to the same information at
the same time in order that, as one slime mould, it can then move towards
food or away from danger, like a snake or a slug.

Is your place of work, or your bank, your university or your supermarket
a slime, a slug or a snake? Or all three?

Like the modern global corporation slime moulds can be very long – up
to several metres – have their brains at the periphery and are subject to a
dynamic external environment. Like the global corporation slime moulds
have survival instincts and can gobble up predators and competitors, but
they can also metamorphose into new organisms, chameleon-like.

The disaster for slime moulds is when the integrity of information is
broken; so that one edge does not know what the other edge is thinking,
sensing or doing. Interestingly, touching a slime mould breaks the

Biomimicry: organisations as slime?

The term slime mould embraces a heterogeneous assemblage of organisms. Slime moulds are found worldwide and typically thrive in dark, cool, moist conditions such as prevail on forest floors. Bacteria yeast, moulds, and fungi provide the main source of slime-mould nutrition, although the Plasmodiophorina feed parasitically on the roots of cabbage and other mustard-family plants. The life cycle of a slime mould begins with a spore that has a diameter of 4 to 15 micrometres (1 micrometre equals 0.001 mm, or 0.000039 inch) and that, in the presence of water, releases a small mass of cytoplasm called a swarm cell. It is propelled by whip-like appendages (flagella) until it comes in contact with a surface and puts forth pseudopods (lobes of cellular material) that allow it to creep along. In its creeping phase it resembles an amoeba and is known as a myxamoeba. Both swarm cells and myxamoebae function as sex cells (gametes), and the fusion of two such cells constitutes the reproductive act of myxomycetes that begins the next stage of growth, the plasmodium. As the flagella are permanently retracted, the fertilised cell begins to grow by repeated division of its nuclei. The plasmodium moves gradually in successive waves, creating a characteristic fan shape. A layer of slime, in some species similar to saliva or mucus, covers the whole plasmodium. The most remarkable metamorphosis of the slime moulds occurs next: the growth from the shapeless plasmodium of an intricately organised spore case, or sporangium. Droplets form at the cell wall and coalesce to form a cushion and then a stalk that can grow to be 1.25 cm (0.5 inch) wide and 2.5 cm (1 inch) tall. As the column changes to purple and then black, the sporangium forms at its tip, filled with the dark spores. The sporangium wall dries and disintegrates, allowing air currents or a sudden movement to release the spores and begin the cycle again.

(1994–2002 *Encyclopædia Britannica*)

membrane and kills it, but cutting it allows the separate parts to form discrete entities. A touch sends a different message to a cut. As Steven Johnson says in *Emergence,* 'for scientists trying to understand systems that use relatively simple components to build higher-level intelligence, the slime mould may someday be seen as the equivalent of the finches and tortoises that Darwin observed on the Galapagos Islands'.[189]

Using the concept of bio-mimicry, Alan Feest predicted that there would be multiple breakdowns and accidents in the newly privatised British Rail in 1997. He was correct and we have seen delays costing millions to the British economy and the loss of many lives. Reducing organisations to their component parts and then asking them to compete is a recipe for absolute and real chaos. In colloquial terms, one hand does not know what the other hand is doing as the vision and values are confused and information is partial and incomplete. Unless all parts of a complex adaptive system, such as a national rail network, are singing from the same hymn sheet it will not work smoothly.

The application of complexity theory to corporate responsibility thinking is designed to inform on the relationship between people and people and people and planet in order to match information to purpose.

Let us return to soap, to the world's best selling soap: Dove, made by Unilever. If the objective is to keep clean, to provide a product that both cleans and delights and to have the least possible ecological footprint, how might we assure ourselves that Dove is the one?

The surviving organisation is now inside-out, with its intelligence on the outside. Central control is possible for a short while but eventually the organisation as an organism will be eaten alive. The global neural networks that have been established do not allow for complacency and the state of the planet only allows us a short space of time to bring our corporations into line with our spiritual, emotional and rational instincts.

The only way to model the future is through an honest examination of the complexities present in any situation. The 20 questions posed in Chapter 6 are based on the study of complexity in the natural sciences, but these thoughts have been mirrored in spiritual learning for many centuries. We are now entering an age where we can model the complexities of life using linear and non-linear learning. This will give us three perspectives: the rational scientific, the helicopter overview and a sense of the connectivities and convivialities that make up the universe in which the world exists. These three symbiotic perspectives will help us see an integrated whole (hole). But first we need people working in discrete professions and intellectual areas to adopt a culture of humility, conviviality and action.

CHAPTER 6

Modelling Corporate Responsibility Situations

Raising a Ladder to the Moon has argued that in order to solve some of the problems created by globalisation (specifically concerned with sustainability and corporate responsibility) we must see the world in the light of its complexities, connectivities and convivialities. This requires the adoption of a culture of humility and conviviality; humility so that we can be in awe of the relationship between people and planet, and conviviality so that we can communicate in peace and equanimity.

'Raising a ladder to the moon' was a metaphor used to describe the immensity of the task of laying the first trans-Atlantic telegraph cable at the end of the nineteenth century. It has been used in this book to illuminate the challenges and opportunities that are inherent in the development of corporations as socially and environmentally responsible 'citizens' at the beginning of the twenty-first century.

The book has been experiential, analytical and I hope full of paradox and surprise. Complexity throws up the unexpected.

I have argued that conventional approaches to corporate responsibility often do not provide solutions to long-standing problems. This is because there is a failure to understand five issues:

- The observer is a powerful determinant of what is seen.
- Altruism is a social, not a personal, characteristic.
- Our corporations are self-organising complex adaptive systems, but, like cities, we try to tie them down, to concretise them, by attempting to rationalise their purpose.
- We and our organisations form a connected community.
- 'Seeing' complexity requires an infinite variety of views, which have three characteristics:
  - awe, love, faith and beauty, which requires trust

–   the scientific method, which requires analytical rigour
–   context, which requires an attitude of mind that can sense the connections between things, between events and between spaces.

The premises for adopting an alternative approach are:

•   There have been significant negative unintended consequences of the increase in the global population and the development of technology, particularly over the last 100 years or so.
•   Human systems seem to be out of kilter with natural systems.
•   Humans have learnt that the world may not be as it has seemed to be in the machine age.
•   Humans need to learn humility towards each other and their environment.
•   Natural systems and our own capabilities continually surprise us.
•   Social systems and organisation are disrupted by unpredicted events that cause significant hardship to people.
•   By modelling complexity we can begin to see emergent patterns that may help us find solutions that we had not even dreamt of.

Meditations

I have in mind several corporate responsibility situations that deserve examination. They are commonly posed conundrums. Over the last 20 years I have posed them to a wide variety of groups including 10-year-old school children, doctoral engineering students, senior business executives, public policy makers and civil society activists. They are designed as exercises in learning by bypassing classically imposed approaches to understanding.

The meditation is in the pondering, with an open mind, a product or an organisation listed. It is a good idea to start with two simple exercises in personal connectivity:

•   First, focus on your breathing. As you breathe in think: where has this air come from? Where has it been? As you breathe out think: where is this air going? Who or what am I giving it to? Whose air is it anyway?
•   Second, stand up, close your eyes, hold out your arms and think: I am a tree. As you stand, think. What sort of tree am I? Where am I? Am I alone

or with other trees? What is happening to my tree? What is happening in my tree? Do I, as a tree, have any rights or responsibilities?

The idea of these simple exercises, which I have practised all over the world with thousands of people, in all sorts of formal and informal situations, is to focus the mind on any thought that comes along. It opens the mind to all sorts of new possibilities. This is at the heart of meditations on the complexities of life.

- Third, approach the following products and organisations with an open mind. The primary situation is summed up as follows: 'I am going to give you a socially derived product. What is it? What is it made of? How is it used? Where do its constituent ingredients come from? What are the constituent parts of the product, its packaging and its promotion? Can you consider it in the light of its social and environmental life cycle and consider its social and environmental impact?'
  - _Dove soap_. To continue one of the themes of this book I have chosen this Unilever product because of it global ubiquity and its relationship with primary human concerns of cleanliness and ageing. I have also chosen it because of its direct connection with another theme of this book: water. Now, start in another space and focus on Unilever: as much a 'thing' as its manufactured products.
  - _Big Mac burger_. Again this is globally ubiquitous and has been referred to elsewhere in the book, as has McDonald's. Also, again food is a primary concern to humans. McDonald's: again, as much a 'thing' as its manufactured products.

The products and organisations listed here can be viewed as complex adaptive systems in themselves or part of such systems. As such they are liable to transformation. They are held together by energies and connectivities based on social and natural processes.

You can call on your own knowledge, the promotion of the product and organisations in its wrapping, any published information, and then any unanswered questions. When you or your group have painted a rich picture of the situation, reassess the model by asking the following 20 questions, which are derived from complexity theory. They are not definitive, and some of them may or may not be useful. But they are meant as a guide, as a series of signposts to new ideas. It is hoped that by considering them all, the unexpected will occur in your mind and in the minds of the people you are problem-solving with.

But remember: 'Seeing' complexity requires an infinite variety of views, which have three characteristics:

- awe, love, faith and beauty, which requires trust
- the scientific method, which requires analytical rigour
- context, which requires an attitude of mind that can sense the connections between things, between events and between spaces.

Twenty questions to ask in modelling the complexities of corporate responsibility

Planet: sustainability questions

1. How is the natural environment viewed and represented? (In other words, how are environmental resources categorised?)
2. Are environmental resources viewed as public or private?
3. What will be the effect of the current situation on future generations?

People: stakeholder ethical questions

4. How active or passive have the actors been, and how have they been engaged?
5. How is respect for diversity, otherness and difference represented?

People: humility and ethical questions

6. Has as much information as possible been gathered? If not, where are the deficits?
7. What will the consequences of any assessment be?
8. How easy will it be to reassess and grow the model?

Learning, unlearning, networks and action: complexity questions

9. How open has the approach been?
10. Does the rich picture of the situation present a whole that is radically different from the sum of the individual parts?
11. How have the relationships, interactions, relativities and connectivities between the parts been represented in the model?
12. Are there any non-linear emergent patterns?
13. Are there any surprises?
14. What is the relationship of information and energy between this model and the external environment? And where are the points of porosity?
15. Where is the greatest uncertainty in the model?
16. How has the model adapted over time past? (In other words, how have we got to this point?)
17. How have the observers affected the model? (In other words, what assumptions have been made in order to reach this point?)
18. How has the model affected the observer's perceptions of the situation?
19. Have new perceptions been fed back into the model?
20. Is it clear that this model is complex: that it is not simple or simply complicated?

* * * *

Now wash and go out for dinner. This is how the world is.
Light a candle, and sit back and wait.

Acknowledgements

Grateful acknowledgement is given to the Random House Group Limited for permission to use the extract from *An Evil Cradling* by Brian Keenan, published by Hutchinson.

My greatest acknowledgements are to people who have inspired me to think again: to learn and unlearn as this book says we all must. Some of these people are friends, some are people I have met in conversations along the way, some have come to me in their books.

If I had a select bibliography that has influenced the writing of this book it would be:

Empire, Michael Hardt and Antonio Negri (2000) Harvard University Press.

Synchronicity, Joseph Jaworski (1996) Berrett-Koehler, San Francisco.

States of Grace, Charlene Spretnak (1993) Harper Collins.

SQ; Spiritual Intelligence, Danah Zohar and Ian Marshall (2000) Bloomsbury, London.

The Saturated Self, Kenneth J. Gergen (1991) Basic Books, New York.

The Emperor's Nightingale, Robert Monks (1998) Perseus, UK.

Cities For A Small Planet, Richard Rogers and Philip Gumuchdjian (1997) Faber and Faber, London.

Country of my Skull, Antje Krog (1998) Cape.

Emergence, Steven Johnson (2001) Penguin, London.

Globalisation And Its Discontents, Joseph Stiglitz (2002) Allen Lane, London.

Conceptual Foundations For Multi-Disciplinary Thinking, Steven Jay Kline (1995) Stanford University Press.

From my wife I learn every day. Louise, a community social worker, returns every day with individual's stories and her frustrations with the inadequacies of public policy and social services in the world's fourth largest economy to deal with the most fundamental issues. From my teenage daughters, Sophie and Cleo, I hear about peer pressure and the demands of the consumer economy. They manage to stand straight and be proud of who they are. Thanks also to Steve Kitson, a post-trauma surgeon, who has talked me through the intricacies of the brain; to Mark Moody-Stuart for time to talk; to Andrew Grant for showing me sun and weather maps as a guide for social spaces – and cities; to Catherine Lumley, a palliative counsellor based in a hospital in Sydney, for trying to put humanity into medicine; to Mark Swilling and Eve Anneke for showing me whales, South Africa, patience, perseverance and transformation and to Franklin Adams who showed me round Khayolistsha township; to Rob McClaughlin for building boats; to Ruth Thomas, Gill Coleman and Deborah Leipziger for kindness in the face of adversity; to John Benington for being straight and supportive. And to Alan Feest for showing me slime mould and finding time to cast an ecologist's eye over the text. I thank my publisher at Palgrave, Stephen Rutt, for his infinite patience.

I have met many people with real power over the last 30 years in my work as a researcher, writer and producer of books and films for universities and television as well as in a previous career in business and management. They include senior government ministers and public servants around the world, as well as civil society activists and business people. Three things differentiate the powerful from the rest: they can focus and they work harder – and they all crave power. You have to want it to get it, and those that get it are not necessarily the best leaders, managers or human beings. I have met very, very few powerful people whom I felt I trusted with my soul. I have met ordinary people that I have trusted with my heart and soul. Trust not our largest organisations, because as complex adaptive systems they are designed, like slime mould, to survive against the odds.

Malcolm McIntosh
Bath, England
January 2003

Notes

1. McIntosh, M. and Thomas, R. (2001) *Global Companies in the Twentieth Century: Selected Archival Histories*, Vol. V, Cable & Wireless, item 7. Routledge, London.

2. Stiglitz, J. (2002) *Globalisation and its Discontents*, p. 248. Penguin/ Allen Lane, Harmondsworth.

3. Kline, S. J. (1995) *Conceptual Foundations for Multi-Disciplinary Thinking*, p. xiii. Stanford University Press, Stanford, CA.

4. Bateson, G. (1972) *Steps to an Ecology of the Mind*, p. 462. Chandler, San Francisco, CA.

5. Senge, P. (1996) in the Introduction to J. Jaworski, *Synchronicity*, p. 11. Berrett-Koehler, San Francisco, CA.

6. For more on this subject see Easlea, B. (1983) *Fathering the Unthinkable: Masculinity, Scientists and the Nuclear Race*. Pluto, London and Sydney.

7. McIntosh, M. (1986) *Japan Re-Armed*. Frances Pinter, London.

8. Collins, J. C. and Porras, J. I. (1996) *Built To Last*. Century, London.

9. Ibid. p. 4.

10. McIntosh and Thomas (2001) op. cit.

11. Chalmers, M. (1985) *Paying for Defence: Military Spending and British Decline*. Pluto, London and Sydney.

12. See, for instance, Rogers, P. F. (2000) *Politics in the Next 50 Years: The Changing Nature of International Conflict*. University of Bradford, Department of Peace Studies.

13. Soros, G. (1998) *The Crisis of Global Capitalism*, p. xxiii. Little Brown, London.

14. Rees, M. (2002) 'Our biophilic universe and its future', *RSA Journal*, December, pp. 48–9.

15. Ibid.

16. See, for instance, Hardt, M. and Negri, A. (2000) *Empire,* Harvard University Press, Cambridge, MA; Giddens, A. (2001) *The Global Third Way Debate,* Polity, Cambridge, UK; and Castells, M. (1996) *The Rise of the Network Society*, Blackwell, Oxford.

17. See, for instance, Lyotard, J.-F. (1979) *The Postmodern Condition: A Report on Knowledge*, Manchester University Press, Manchester; Glover, J. (2001) *Humanity: A Moral History of the Twentieth Century,* Pimlico, London; Krog, A. (1998) *Country of My Skull,* Cape, London; Pirsig, R. M. (1974) *Zen and the Art of Motorcycle Maintenance: An Enquiry into Values*, Vintage, London; and Heartney, E. (2002) *Movements In Modern Art: Postmodernism*, Tate Publishing, London.

18. For a brief overview of the MBA curriculum in the twenty-first century see Chowdhury, S. *et al.* (2000) *Management 21C,* Pearson, London.

19. Eliot, T. S. (1944) *Four Quartets*. Faber and Faber, London.

20. Gergen, K. J. (2000) *The Saturated Self*, p. ix. Basic Books, New York.

21. According to Drugscope 30–40 per cent of 15–16-year-olds use cannabis regularly in the United Kingdom. According to the UK government, one in nine 16-year-olds admit using drugs every day. The United Kingdom has the highest level of use of hard drugs in Europe, yet it has the toughest laws on drug use.

22. <www.google.com>.

23. Frankl, V. (1959) *Man's Search For Meaning*. Pocket Books, New York; Bettelheim, B. (1952) *Surviving*. Thames and Hudson, London.

24. Ibrahim, A. (1990) *Echoes From Africa*, audio CD, Enja; and *Township One More Time* (1998), EMI.

25. Monks, Robert A. G. (1997) *The Emperor's Nightingale*. Perseus, UK.

26. <www.benjaminzander.com>.

27. Annan, K. (2000) 'The global compact', in M. McIntosh, *Visions of Ethical Business 2*. FT Management and PricewaterhouseCoopers, London.

28. Hardt, M. and Negri, A. (2000) *Empire*. Harvard University Press, Cambridge, MA.

29. Bauman, Z. (1993) *Postmodern Ethics*. Blackwell, Oxford.
30. Birch, D. (2001) 'Corporate citizenship: rethinking business beyond corporate social responsibility', in M. McIntosh and J. Andriof, *Perspectives on Corporate Citizenship*, pp. 53–65. Greenleaf, Sheffield.
31. Ridderstale, J. and Nordstrom, K. (2000) *Funky Business: Talent Makes Capital Dance*, p. 10. Financial Times/Prentice Hall, London.
32. Barber, B. (2001) 'How to make society civil and democracy strong', in A. Giddens, *The Global Third Way Debate,* p. 269. Polity, Cambridge.
33 The Millennium Poll on Corporate Social Responsibility (2001). Environics International Ltd, Toronto <www.environics.net/eil>.
34. Hawken, P. (1994) *The Ecology of Commerce*: *A Declaration of Sustainability*. Weidenfeld and Nicholson, London.
35. Soros, G. (1998) *The Crisis of Global Capitalism*, p. xvi. Little, Brown, London.
36. Barnet, R. J. and Cavanagh, J. (1994) *Global Dreams*, p. 21. Simon and Schuster, London.
37. <www.unglobalcompact.org>.
38. Hertz, N. (2001) *The Silent Takeover*, Random House, London; Klein, N. (2001) *No Logo*, Flamingo, London; Welford, R. (1997) *Hijacking Environmentalism,* Earthscan, London; Korten, D. C. (1995) *When Corporations Rule the World*, Earthscan, London.
39. McIntosh, M., Thomas, R., Leipziger, D. and Coleman, R. (2003) *Living Corporate Citizenship*. FT and Prentice Hall, London.
40. McIntosh, M. (1993) 'Introduction' in *Good Business? Case Studies in Corporate Social Responsibility*. Centre for Social Management and New Consumer, University of Bristol, Policy Press, Bristol.
41. See *Encyclopaedia Britannica* (2002) and Heater, D. (1999) *What Is Citizenship?* Polity, Cambridge.
42. Henderson, D. (2001) 'Misguided virtue'. NZ Business Roundtable, June <www.nzbr.org.nz>.
43. <www.cw.com/community>.
44. <www.enron.com/corp/whoweare>.
45. <www.unilever.com>.
46. Otherwise known as soft porn.
47. Doward, J. (2002) 'Lord of the lap dance'. *Observer*, London, 3 February.

48. Egan, J. and Wilson D. (2002) *Private Business: Public Battleground.* Palgrave, Basingstoke.
49. See, for instance, Barnett, R. J. and Cavanagh, J. (1994) *Global Dreams.* Simon and Schuster, London; and Brown, P. and Lauder, H. (2001) *Capitalism And Social Progress.* Palgrave, Basingstoke.
50. <www.unilever.com>.
51. Ibid.
52. Interview with J. K. Galbraith by R. Cornwall. *Independent*, 1 July 2002. London.
53. <www.unglobalcompact.org>.
54. For Coutts, see <www.Coutts.com>.
55. Newbold, Y. (2002) 'The changing language in the boardroom', in M. McIntosh, *Visions of Ethical Business.* FT/PricewaterhouseCoopers, London.
56. The discussions took place in London and New York in 2001 with directors and chairs of boards of companies from all sectors.
57. McIntosh, M. (1990) *Managing Britain's Defence.* Macmillan, Basingstoke.
58. McIntosh and Thomas (2001) op. cit.
59. Ibid.
60. Hobsbawm, E. (1994) *Age of Extremes.* Michael Joseph, London.
61. See, for instance, the King Report into Corporate Governance, South Africa.
62. Beck, U. (2000) *What Is Globalisation?* p. 11. Polity, Cambridge.
63. Globucate: to communicate all over the world at any time not knowing or caring where your message bounces off or from before it flies from your phone to your conversationee.
64. Morgan, G. (1997) *Images of Organisations*, p 378. Sage, London.
65. Hutton, W. (2002) *The World We're In*, Little Brown, London; Friedman, T. (1999) *The Lexus and the Olive Tree*, Farrar, Strauss & Giroux, New York; Micklelthwait, J. and Wooldridge, A. (2000) *A Future Perfect*, Heinemann, London.
66. Hutton, W. (1996) *The State We're In*, p. xxvii, Vintage, London.
67. Micklethwait, J. and Wooldridge, A. (2000) *A Future Perfect*, p. 335. Heinemann, London
68. Conrad, P. (2002) 'The A to Z of Britney Spears'. *Sunday Times*, Review, Sunday 17 February.

69. Scholte, J. A. (2001) 'Globalisation, governance and corporate citizenship', *Journal of Corporate Citizenship*, No. 1, Spring, pp. 15–23.
70. Annan, K. (1999) *The Global Compact*. <www.unglobal compact.org>.
71. See for instance G. Salaman (2001) *Understanding Business Organisations*, p. 172. Open University/Routledge, London.
72. See for instance McIntosh *et al.* (2002) *Living Corporate Citizenship*, Chapter 4, FT/Pearson, London.
73. <http://www.rspb.org.uk>.
74. <http://www.uia.org/>. See also Bendell, J. (ed.) (2000) 'Introduction: working with stakeholder pressure for sustainable development', in *Terms for Endearment: Business, NGOs and Sustainable Development*. Greenleaf, Sheffield.
75. Willets, P. (1998) 'Political globalisation and the impact of NGOs upon transnational companies', in J. Mitchell, *Companies in a World of Conflict*. Royal Institute for International Affairs and Earthscan, London.

    For NGOs to be considered for consultative status by the UN they must be non-profit making, non-violent, non-criminal and not directed against a particular government. International federations of parties and groups showing a general international concern with human rights are accepted. ECOSOC (UN Economic and Social Council) Resolution 1996/31, 25 July 1996.
76. Bendell, J. (ed.) (2000) *Terms for Endearment: Business, NGOs and Sustainable Development*. Greenleaf, Sheffield.
77. Drucker, P. F. (1999) *Management Challenges for the 21st Century*. Butterworth Heinemann, Oxford and Manchester University Press.
78. Covey, S. R. (1989) *The Seven Habits of Highly Effective People*. Simon & Schuster, London.
79. Chowdhury, S. (2000) 'Management 21C'. *Financial Times*.
80. <www.scottbader.com>. See also Hoe, S. (1978) *The Man Who Gave His Company Away*, Allison Printers, Wollaston, Northants; Schumacher, E. F. (1973) *Small Is Beautiful*, Blond & Briggs, London.
81. Senge, P. *et al.* (1999) *The Dance of Change*, pp. 3–4. Nicholas Brealey, London.
82. Whitley, R. (1999) *Divergent Capitalisms*, p. 5. Oxford University Press, Oxford.

83.   Huntingdon, S. P. (1997) *The Clash of Civilisations and the Remaking of World Order*. Simon & Schuster, London.

84.   For a more detailed explanation of the Global Eight, see McIntosh *et al.* (2002) *Living Corporate Citizenship,* FT/Pearson, London.

85.   Soros, G. (1998) *The Crisis of Global Capitalism*, p. xxxiii. Little, Brown, London.

86.   <www.gov.za/awards/mbekiafrican.htm>.

87.   *Weekend Argus*, 17 August 2002, p. 17.

88.   Osborn, A. (2002) 'New from McDonald's: the McAfrika burger'. *Guardian*, 24 August.

89.   <www.mcdonalds.com>.

90.   See Scholte, op. cit., pp. 15–23.

91.   Hawthorne, P. (1996) 'The new managers'. *TIME International*, 15 January.

92.   <www.mcdonalds.com/social/>.

93.   <www.anglo-american.com>.

94.   Visser, W. and Sunter, C. (2002) *Beyond Reasonable Greed*. Human & Rousseau Tafelberg, Cape Town.

95.   Swilling, M. and Russell, B. (2002) *The Size and Scope of the Non-Profit Sector in South Africa*, p. viii, quoting A. Habib, Director of the Centre for Civil Society, University of Natal. Universities of Natal and Witwatersrand, South Africa,

96.   Ibid., pp. 4 and viii.

97.   See, for instance, the country's largest financial institution. Old Mutual's *Corporate Citizenship Report 2001* says: 'AIDS is undoubtedly the biggest single threat facing South Africa'.

98.   Visser and Sunter, op. cit.

99.   Barthes, R. (1993) 'Soap powders and detergents', in *Mythologies*, trans. A. Lavers, pp. 36–8. Vintage, London.

100. Hardt, M. and Negri, A. (2000) *Empire*, p. 150. Harvard University Press, Cambridge, MA.

101. Handy, C. (1998) 'The real challenge to business', in M. McIntosh, *Visions of Ethical Business*. FT/PricewaterhouseCoopers. <www.business-minds.com>.

102. <www.bbc.co.uk/i/hi/business/1952405.stm>.

103. Fitzgerald, N. (2000) 'Whose future is it anyway?' 30 March at Dublin Castle. <www.unilever.com>.

104. For 'deconstructing the boundaries of the nation-state', see Hardt and Negri, op. cit.
105. <www.Unilever.com>.
106. Ibid.
107. Master, M. (2002) *Just Another Commodity?* (quoting from M. Barlow and T. Clarke, *Blue Gold: The Fight to Stop the Corporate Theft of the World's Water*). New Press, Canada.
108. Rees, S. (2002) Metropolitan conversations at Manley. Oral communication.
109. Patten, C. (2000) *Respect for the Earth Discussion*, p. 112. BBC Radio 4 Reith Lectures/Profile Books, London.
110. Capra, F. (1982) *The Turning Point*, p. 25. Flamingo, London.
111. IUCN, UNEP, WWF (1991) *Caring for the Earth*, p. 8. Earthscan, London.
112. Hobsbawm, E. (1994) *The Age of Extremes: The Shorter Twentieth Century 1914–1991*, p. 569. Michael Joseph, London.
113. Ponting, C. (1991) *A Green History of The World*, p. 161. Penguin, Harmondsworth.
114. Lyotard, J.-F. (1979) *The Postmodern Condition: A Report on Knowledge*. Manchester University Press, Manchester.
115. Heartney, E. (2002) *Postmodernism*, Tate Publishing, London.
116. <www.unilever.com>.
117. Jardine, M. and Love, M. (1971) 'Don't go near the water', on *Surf's Up*. Capitol Records, EMI.
118. Coppola, F. F. (1979) *Apocalypse Now*.
119. Conrad, J. (1902/1995) *Heart of Darkness*, p. 20. Penguin, London.
120. Drucker, P. F. (1999) *Management Challenges for the 21st Century*, Butterworth Heinemann, Oxford and MA; Barnet, R. L. and Cavanagh, J. (1994) *Global Dreams*, Simon & Schuster, London. Hobsbawm, E. (1994) *The Age of Extremes: The Shorter Twentieth Century 1914–1991*, Michael Joseph, London.
121. Ponting, op. cit.
122. Barlow, M. and Clarke, T. (2002) *Blue Gold: The Fight to Stop the Corporate Theft of the World's Water*. New Press, Canada.
123. Giddens, A. (1998) *The Third Way*, p. 57. Polity, London.
124. UNEP (2002) *Global Environment Outlook 3*. UNEP/Earthscan. <www.UNEP.org>.

125. WWF (2002) *Living Planet Report 2002*. <www.wwf.org>.

126. McIntosh, C. (1998) 'The good things and the bad things in the world', in *Visions of Ethical Business 1*, p. 17. FT Management/ PricewaterhouseCoopers/Council on Economic Priorities. London and New York.

127. <www.unilever.com>.

128. Beck, U. (1991) *Ecological Enlightenment*, trans. M. Ritter (1995). Humanities Press, New Jersey.

129. Senghor, L. S. (1976) *Prose and Poetry*. Heinemann, London (quoted in D. F. Murphy (2001) *African Enterprises and the Global Compact: Adding Value through Human Relationships*. ILO, Tunis, Tunisia). This article can also be found in the *Journal of Corporate Citizenship*, No. 11, June 2003.

130. Bateson, G. (1972) *Steps to an Ecology of the Mind*, p. 462. Chandler, San Francisco, CA.

131. Andriof, J. and Waddock, S. (2002) *Unfolding Stakeholder Thinking*, p. 20. Greenleaf, Sheffield.

132. Andriof, J. (2001) 'Patterns of stakeholder partnership nuilding', in J. Andriof and M. McIntosh, *Perspectives on Corporate Citizenship*, p. 215. Greenleaf, Sheffield.

133. Bohm, D. (1980) *Wholeness and The Implicate Order*, Taylor & Francis, London; Rayner, A. D. M. (2002) 'Inclusionality: an immersive philosophy of environmental relationships', in A. Winnet, *ICE Proceedings*, Macmillan, Basingstoke.

134. Monks, op. cit.; Stewart, I. (1990) *Does God Play Dice?* Blackwell, Oxford.

135. Cilliers, P. (1998) *Complexity and Postmodernism*, Routledge, London; Swilling, M. (2002) *Two Cultures: The Intellectual Basis for Greater Collaboration Between the Sciences and Humanities in the Twenty-first Century*, opening address for the workshop on the Origins of Humanity and the Diffusion of Human Populations in Africa, 17–19 September, Stellenbosch, South Africa. Convened by the Africa Human Genome Initiative.

136. Casti, J. (2002) 'BizSim: the world of business in a box'. <www.santafe.edu/sfi/education/csss/files02/casti.pdf>; Monks, op. cit.; Morgan, G. (1997) *Images of Organisations*, Sage, London; Hatch, M. J. (1997) *Organisation Theory: Modern Symbolic and Postmodern Perspectives*. Oxford University Press, Oxford.

137. Reason, P. and Goodwin, B. (1999) 'Towards a science of qualities in organisations: lessons from complexity theory and postmodern biology'. *Concepts and Transformations*, Vol. 4, No. 3, pp. 281–317.

138. Blockley, D., Farinha, F. and Bento, J. (2002) *A Systems Approach to the Computer Aided Design of Reinforced Concrete Structures.* <www.civil.ist.utl.pt/joao/pdf/DesModels.pdf 26/11/02>.

139. See McIntosh, M. *et al.* (1998) op. cit.

140. de Geus, A. (1997) *The Living Company: Growth, Learning and Longevity In Business,* pp. 7–19. Nicholas Brealey, London.

141. Capra, F. (1988) *Uncommon Wisdom: Conversations With Remarkable People.* Flamingo, London.

142. Cilliers, P. (1998) *Complexity and Postmodernism.* Routledge, London.

143. *Economist*, 5 October 2002, pp. 96 and 99.

144. Gladwell, M. (2000) *The Tipping Point: How Little Things can Make a Big Difference.* Little, Brown, London.

145. Shaw, G. B. (1903/2000) 'Maxims for revolutionaries', postscript to *Man and Superman.* Penguin, Harmondsworth.

146. Cilliers, op. cit. pp. 2–3.

147. Ibid.

148. Swilling, M. (2002) op. cit.

149. Schossler, E. (2002) *Fast Food Nation.* Penguin, London.

150. Fowles, J. (1998) *Daniel Martin.* Vintage, London.

151. de Geus, op. cit.; Collins, J. C. and Porras, J. I. (1996) *Built To Last.* Century, New York.

152. Kaufman, Stuart, referenced in David Berreby, 'Between order and chaos', <www.strategy-business.com>. 9 October 2002.

153. Zohar, D. (1997) *Rewiring the Corporate Brain.* Berrett-Koehler, San Francisco, CA.

154. Bauman, Z., op. cit.

155. Lyotard, J.-F. (1979) *The Postmodern Condition: A Report on Knowledge.* Manchester University Press, Manchester.

156. Based on Swilling, M., op. cit., and Cilliers, P., op. cit. pp. 139–40.

157. See McIntosh, M. *et al.* (2002) *Living Corporate Citizenship.* FT/Pearson, London.

158. Schumacher College <schumacher@org.uk>. Schumacher, E. F. (1952) *Small Is Beautiful.* Blond & Briggs, London.

159. For the Global Compact, see <www.unglobalcompact.org> and for Melbourne see <http://65.214.34.30/un/gc/unweb.nsf/content/Australia01.htm>.

160. Rogers, R. (1997) *Cities for a Small Planet*, pp. 2 and 25. Faber and Faber, London.

161. Morgan, G. (1997) *Images of Organisations*, p. 265. Sage, London.

162. Ibid., p. 269.

163. For an explanation of the history and origins of the Global Compact go to <www.unglobalcomapct,org> or see Chapter 6 in M. McIntosh *et al.* (2002) *Living Corporate Citizenship*, FT/Pearson, London.

164. Casti, J., adapted from 'Would-be worlds'. *Encyclopaedia Britannica*, 1994–2002.

165. Berreby, D. (2002) *Between Chaos and Order: What Complexity Theory Can Teach Business.* <www.strategy-business.com>.

166. Monks, op. cit., p. 19.

167. <www.nancho.net/newchau/cpmonks.html>.

168. Shiva, V. (2000) 'Respect for the Earth'. BBC Radio 4 Reith Lecture 2000, post-lecture discussion. <www.BBC.co.uk>.

169. Browne, Sir J. (2000). Post-lecture discussion, BBC Radio 4 Reith Lecture 2000. <www.BBC.co.uk>.

170. Monks, op. cit., p. 190.

171. Ward, B. (1979) *Progress for a Small Planet*, p. 10. Penguin, London.

172. Maathai, W. (1995) 'A view from the grassroots', in T. Wakeford and M.Walters, *Science for the Earth*, pp. 279, 291. Wiley, London.

173. Snow, C. P. (1959/1993) *Two Cultures*. 1959 Rede Lecture. Cambridge University Press, Cambridge, UK.

174. Morgan, op. cit. p. 279.

175. Worldwatch Institute (2000/2001) *Vital Signs*. Earthscan, London.

176. Bell, S. and Morse, S. (1999) *Sustainability Indicators*, p. 125. Earthscan, London.

177. Rogers, R. and Gumuchdjian, P. (1997) *Cities for a Small Planet*, pp. 5 and 169. Faber and Faber, London.

178. Bell and Morse, op cit., p. 126.

179. <www.earthscan.co.uk>.

180. Holliday, C. O. *et al.* (2002) *Walking the Talk*. Greenleaf, Sheffield.

181. Weizsacker, E. *et al.* (1998) *Factor Four: Doubling Wealth, Halving Resource Use*. Earthscan, London.
182. Stahel, W. (2002) *Complexity, Technology, Sustainability*. <www.inesglobalcom>.
183. Gore, A. (2000) *Earth in the Balance*. Earthscan, London.
184. Monks, op. cit. p. 190.
185. Senge, P. (1996) 'Introduction' to J. Jaworski, *Synchronicity*, p. 11. Berrett-Koehler, San Francisco, CA.
186. Ibid., p. 12.
187. Casti, J. (2002), op. cit.
188. Feest, A. <www.bristol.ac.uk>.
189. Johnson, S. (2001) *Emergence: The Connected Lives of Ants, Brains, Cities and Software*, p. 11. Penguin, Harmondsworth.

Index